Advice and Cautions for Independent Publishing Authors

The Compiled Indie Publishing Subjects of Jim Lowrance

By: James M. Lowrance © 2012

2

Advice and Cautions for Independent Publishing Authors

SECTION ONE

Are Revenue Sharing Article/Content Publishing Sites Beneficial?

Legitimate Opportunities for Authors

To all of the sincere, hard-working authors and content contributors who are simply looking for honest websites and online outlets to enter into successful, long-term relationship with.

TABLE OF CONTENTS (SECTION ONE):

INTRODUCTION - SECTION ONE:

The revenue-sharing content website industry has grown into a multi-billion dollar a year online business. These are websites (sites) that offer interesting or needed information to readers who visit their online pages but who at the same time, sell advertising units, which appear as ads around each piece of content they display (i.e. articles, audios, photos or videos).

In many cases these ads are the Google Adsense type. If authors or content contributors want to share in the revenue generated by these type sites they can register for an Adsense account and they will be supplied with their own unique account number, once approved. This allows Google to track the clicks on ads displayed around content they have submitted to websites and to be paid their percent of the revenue advertisers pay for those clicks on ads purchased by them. It is an effective and precise method of offering advertising online and to pay both the administration and content contributors at revenue-sharing websites. (NOTE: Google has strict policy against "click fraud" and they are well-equipped to track down unlawfully gained Adsense revenue.)

Some websites pay their contributors based on the numbers of clicks their content receives, rather than for numbers of clicks on ad-units and this can be something like $1.50 or $2.00 per 1,000 page-views on their combined pieces of content or paid on each individual piece of content that reaches this many page-views. Contributors are usually asked to provide a bank account for direct deposit of payments to them or they are asked to obtain a PayPal account for earned revenue deposits to be paid into. Other sites pay upfront amounts for content they accept from contributors or a combination of upfront payments and ongoing ad revenue shares. Yet other sites actually pay base salaries to their contributors, who in this case are often referred to as "Editors" or "Guides".

This system can be very beneficial to content contributors but much of this depends on what websites one decides to register-with and the level of quality content submissions one has. In some cases, less-reputable or dishonest revenue sharing websites have done disservice to their contributors, by discontinuing revenue-sharing after gleaning massive amounts of content from them.

Others have done disservice by canceling contributor's memberships for bogus reasons or by unethically penalizing the revenue shares of members.

In the chapters that follow, I will address these types of issues and offer recommendations for choosing revenue sharing sites that can be beneficial rather than negative experiences for content contributors.

CHAPTER ONE

My Personal Experience with Revenue Sharing Websites

Beginning in year 2004, I began to write articles online, submitting them to websites that did not offer revenue share opportunities. I however, enjoyed these sites personally and felt that they offered high quality content to readers. My main enjoyment of writing was to share helpful information to readers. In my case, being a medical patient, diagnosed with autoimmune thyroid disease and other co-morbid health disorders, I simply enjoyed sharing any knowledge I was gaining from extensive online searches, with fellow patients.

After a couple of years however, I became interested in submitting articles to revenue sharing sites. I felt that with the fact that visitors could still read articles at no charge and that advertisers actually benefited from this type set up, as well as the sites and content contributors, this was beneficial to each party involved. I have since contributed 100s of online articles to these type sites and I continue to receive revenue share payments from them to date.

I have not gotten wealthy from this venue but it has at times been a nice supplement to my income. I personally have had more success with book and e-book sales; however the contributions I made to content websites, actually trained me toward much better writing and editing skills that I was later able to incorporate into my books (more on book and e-book publishing in CHAPTER FIVE).

I did also have negative experiences with particular content websites. In one case of my canceling my membership with a site, I had contributed approximately 80 articles to a "How-To" type property that shared Adsense revenue with authors who wrote for them. The payments grew to a very nice level and I was being paid from my Google Adsense Account, which was deposited into my bank account, on a fairly regular basis. In order for Google to release Adsense payments, they must reach a $100.00 threshold and mine began reaching this about every other month and so I was obviously pleased and excited. At one point I noticed that my revenue began to accumulate much more slowly and I immediately knew something had changed with one of the sites I was writing for.

In my Adsense account, which allows you to create "channels", meaning individualized viewing of how much revenue each site you contribute-to is generating, I noticed that this 'How-To' site's revenue dropped completely off. It was showing zero revenue week after week, following a period of time when revenue was showing up almost daily.

I contacted the site by email, asking why I was no longer receiving Adsense Revenue shares from my content on their site and they explained that they discontinued sharing the site's revenue with contributors. I asked why they did not inform me of this and they stated that they had sent out a blanket email to all contributors explaining this. I not only did not receive the email but other fellow-writers, whom I knew outside of the site but who also wrote for them also did not receive the notification email. We were able to ascertain that the delay in contributors receiving notifications was so-that the site could continue to glean from them as many more pieces of content as possible before some of the members could cancel their memberships in response to the unfair change.

The site further informed me that their contributor agreement specifies that they could make these type changes "at any time, without notice" but that contributors would be informed and given opportunity to discontinue their contributions should they so decide. I responded by asking the site to remove all of my content from their pages and that if they did not do so, I would be seeking legal action against them and they agreed to do so. I was actually surprised that they did not invite me to take any action I wished and that they would respond with their own legal action but thankfully it did not come to that.

A similar negative experience I had with a content website, sharing revenue with members, involved them not accruing my page-views in my account. The counter remained at zero for an extended period of time after I began publishing dozens of content-pieces. Upon my inquiring with them about it, they pointed out that I failed to complete a particular item of registration, if I remember correctly, having to do with my tax information. It would have seemed logical for them to have let the page-view counter run in the mean time but this was one of many methods they used to hold back contributor revenue.

I supplied the needed information and continued to contribute to the website.

I then experienced a point at which my accumulated revenue, which was only a few dollars, was suddenly rolled back to zero. I again inquired as to why this had occurred and this time, they pointed out that I had not properly selected a prompt on a recent piece of content I published (having to do with categories if I remember correctly) and that the rolled-back revenue was a penalty for this. I saw where other contributors were complaining on other website forums about this content site, saying that they were not being paid for their articles due to being outside of the USA but that they were unaware of this policy (it was stated in their agreement but somewhat vaguely).

You would think that when they submitted all of their information to be paid revenue shares, someone with the site administration would have then emailed them explaining this. Instead, the site did not want to risk not gleaning content from these members and so they remained somewhat elusive regarding the issue.

I ended up canceling my membership with this content site as well but because of about 75 pieces of my content being placed by me, in a particular revenue share category when I published them, they refused to remove them from their site. Almost four years later (all the while, the site earning revenue on my content), I found information stating that the site had changed administration and so I asked them if I could rejoin them as a contributor (the new management sounded promising). They agreed and reopened my account and I began to submit content to them, which reached about 130 new pieces I published on the site.

I also submitted five articles to them under a more exclusive revenue share category and upon reviewing them, an editor informed me that I was no longer a member and he referred to my earlier self-cancellation with the site, from over three years previously. He stated that I could ask that my account be reopened and afterward I could resubmit the exclusive articles (I had already done so and was accepted). I responded by canceling my membership once-again, this-time permanently because my account had not only **already been reinstated** but I was publishing and submitting new articles with them.

This would have been impossible to do without current membership. This was a bad sign in my opinion and I felt I could not trust the site to properly accrue any payments due to me or that if they did begin well with me, they might find a bogus reason at a later date to discontinue my membership or to roll-back my revenue.

I was not willing to degrade my authored work again, on their site, as had occurred in the past. While I hope this will not come across offensive I feel this type of relationship with a content site, in-essence is requiring authors to prostitute their work. This is a term I once heard a fellow-author use on a publishing forum, when referring to some venues writers will accept that degrades their authorship and while it is a blunt statement to use regarding this type issue, I feel it is a legitimate analogy.

Are all content sites involved in the bogus or dishonest type practices, such as those I have described above? Certainly not, in-fact there are many highly-ethical and reputable websites that provide benefit and reasonable respect to contributors as I stated in my introduction.

I am very pleased with one content site in-particular that I have written for, who has been faithful to compute and pay me monthly for page-views that accrue on my content that appears on their pages. I was also impressed with their promptness to communicate with writers and to respond to any problems on the site as they occurred.

I did have issue with one particular editor on the site, who required changes on some of my articles that actually changed the theme and meaning of them however, there were other editors who were very reasonable with their required changes on my submitted content. I do not feel this editor was intentionally trying to enforce her own style onto my articles but rather felt she was doing me a service. Her required changes did however result in exactly that – a change in the original meanings of sections in my articles.

I reported this issue to the administration who defended the actions of the editor and so I respectfully discontinued writing for the site. I actually could have stayed on with them and written for other topics on the site as I had in the past and having had no serious problems with the editors over those.

I felt however that this particular issue was serious enough, that my resigning would possibly help the administration to take the issue of overboard editing requirements more seriously, for the sake of future writers submitting content to that particular topic.

It is not possible to find a site to submit articles or other works of content to, that will be perfect in every respect. It's also possible that I set my own standards for sites I chose to write for, a little too high but some of this came from my previous negative experiences with sites that had serious issues that were not being resolved.

It might also help a content producer, looking for a site to join, to conduct an online search, using the site(s) name(s) in a search engine, to see if there are positive or negative reviews of them being posted.

There are actually websites and blogs whose sole purpose is reviewing websites and providing information regarding their revenue earnings and net worth.

These can provide valuable information when considering websites for participation in.

In the Chapters that follow, I will point out other basic things one should look for, when deciding what type of site(s) they choose to submit their articles and content works to.

CHAPTER TWO

Things to Consider in a Content Revenue Site Contract

Is the agreement a site offers to become a content producer, overly one-sided in their benefit?

While a website certainly has to protect itself when offering content producer agreements, they should also demonstrate that they are interested in helping their members succeed as well. The contracted members are after-all the very life-blood of their website and without them, they also would not succeed. It is typical for example for content sites to warn of canceling memberships, should a content producer plagiarize on their site (stealing content from other sources and republishing it is their own). It is also typical for them to ask members not to spam their site under warning of canceled membership. This would include things such as redirecting links in articles (ones that take readers to other sites for marketing purposes); adding more links than are allowed, within the body of an article and when content producers overly promote themselves in articles.

They also have a right to warn members not to extract their software (illegal hacking), such as parts of their publishing platform, to use on their own sites, or to sell to others. Lastly, they have a right to restrict the use of profanity, bigotry of any kind and obscenity in any form.

What might send up a red flag however in regard to a contributor agreement, are things such as warnings that a member's account can be canceled "at any time and for any reason" or that the site's policies can be changed "at anytime without notice". It would be better for an agreement to state that members can lose membership for legitimate reasons specified and that any changes in the agreement will be updated with a 15 or 30 day notice to contributors. Not having these type terms, does not necessarily mean that a site is not a good venue for a content producer but all of these type things should be evaluated and considered together as a whole when choosing a site to contribute content to.

Another very important consideration is whether or not a content site allows members to retain the copyrights to their submitted content or if it becomes the perpetual, exclusive property of the site.

In some cases, sites require totally original content that has not been published elsewhere, on any other online or in-print source previously. This-too is not necessarily a bad thing and possibly even a positive, as long as the contributor can remove the content or have it removed, in the event they resign with the website or have their membership canceled at some point.

Does the content producer agreement warn of penalties that may occur, even if common or honest mistakes are made by members?

Breaking policies like those I have described in the previous subheading are legitimate reasons for a content producer's membership at a site to be canceled. If however the reasons for losing membership listed include things such as not having logged-in to one's account for 30, 60 or even 90 days, not contributing a certain number of content-pieces within a set amount of time (unless reasonable and achievable) or having improperly categorized an article, these are unreasonably strict policies in my opinion and a strong reason to reconsider joining a site who enforces them.

I mention this because some circumstances are beyond one's control, such as an illness that keeps one from going online for months at a time or a new content producer who inadvertently uses a prompt on a publishing platform incorrectly, as they are learning better publishing skills.

If however the site is one that pays high-level compensation or base salaries, these type requirements are then reasonably required and understandably needed.

To offer an example of a policy a site enforced in their agreement that required me to inquire with them after I published content on their site, had to do with "members clicking on their own articles" (the site paid contributors per page views). Their agreement stated that generating clicks on articles that were not legitimate views by site visitors would result in the immediate and permanent cancellation of a contributor's membership (false clicks). At the same time, the site encouraged contributors to link to other articles on the site they had written (allowing three links on new articles).

I found that linking to my other articles on the site required me to go to my articles-list on the site and to click on those I wanted to link-to, in order to copy and paste the links into new articles.

I wrote to the site administration, to make sure that by my doing this, I was not endangering my membership with the site but I did not receive a response on the inquiry. My suspicion however, is that they would have told me that clicking on one's own links on the site for this purpose was permissible, since it was actually a benefit to them, in helping to increase traffic to other articles on the site. I did wonder however if this scenario had occurred to them and that it might have been a detail that could have been added to that particular term in their content producer agreement. This same type scenario would also apply to authors who copy/paste their article-links at forums or social networks they frequented, to promote their works.

Certainly an author can copy/paste all of their article links on one page and save them as a document-file to avoid unnecessary clicks on their content.

The forethought for doing this type thing however, is not always there when authors are inexperienced or are not offered instruction for doing this, to avoid false click suspicions. This demonstrates that content producer contract terms, are not always as "cut and dried" (as easily adhered-to) as sites would like them to be and that if a contracted member feels they are being unduly reprimanded or wrongly ejected from membership for a violation, they should be given opportunity to offer explanation for their questionable actions. I mention this because in worse-case scenarios dishonest websites have actually resorted to bogus excuses for canceling memberships, in order to retain a contributor's content or to avoid having to pay-out revenue shares due to them.

Does the site have a responsive administration, willing to communicate to the needs, problems or questions of content producers?

Nothing can be more frustrating to a content site member who cannot get the administration to respond to them. Issues that can arise may include things such as seeing content suddenly disappear from one's account and accrued revenue payments not being received.

Other issues may include experiencing bugs in the publishing software that prevents new content from being submitted properly. The site should take interest in these type issues because members who can stay active in contributing content, without these type hindrances, will continue to increase the site's traffic and revenue.

Some content sites are very large and understandably, these types can find difficulty in responding individually to massive numbers of emails. Many remedy this problem by providing a "Questions & Answers" page on their site and/or by providing a contributor's forum, where problems and issues can be discussed with members who have already experienced them and can recommend solutions to newer members (more regarding forums under the next sub-heading).

Is the site lacking good screening of improper content being published on the site?

Another important step a content producer should take is to browse the pages of websites they are considering membership with. Is it reader-friendly? Is the site-layout easy to navigate? Do they allow offensive material on the site?

Does their publishing software offer "word check" (spelling and punctuation corrections)? These type questions have to do with a site's quality and are very important considerations. I personally for example, canceled membership at a content website, due to the increased allowing of religious bigotry and offensive article posts that were commonly being added to their pages by contributors. Many contained material that was close to pornographic and as the site-administration continued to fail in removing this type content, it began to increase and site was no longer reader-friendly overall.

The site obviously wanted to see the most content possible on their pages but increased revenue, versus an eventually degraded reputation for a website, is not a good trade in my opinion. Of course this is a different story if a site actually rallies in this type of content but in this case, a content producer will be able to recognize this fact and add it into their considerations in deciding whether or not to join the site.

The same is true of content site forums that degrade over time due to lack of moderation. Are forum members attacking each other on the forum?

Are offensive posts in-general being allowed? These are important questions as well because the intent of content site forums should be to exchange needed or interesting information, while respect for fellow-members is also being demonstrated. The forum should reflect the same quality and theme as the site in-general displays in the content they allow to be published.

CHAPTER THREE

Getting your own Blog or Website to Generate Revenue

Another method for publishing content and adding monetization to it via Google Adsense or through other paid advertising venues is to be set up with a personal blog or website. While it's true that starting from scratch with a new site can take time to promote and to gain substantial traffic (visitors), it does have its advantages. One advantage is that you are in-control as the site administrator and you can choose the template for it (general design and theme) and you can design the overall layout of the site, to your liking. You may also choose to add a forum to the site if your hosting company (provider of your website publishing tools) provides this option or allows readers to post comments beneath the articles you publish on it. Another advantage is that you can own the domain of your website or blog (the registered online address of it). This makes the site's name and online address uniquely yours and prevents anyone else from registering the same domain that you become owner of (may need to be renewed yearly).

This would also give you the liberty to provide readers visiting your site, with the type of content you decide to publish on it, whether it's one subject or multiple ones.

In the case of a blog, some site-owners actually publish stories about their selves and other information with a more personal type touch to it and others actually make their blogs into life-journals that document interesting occurrences in their lives (i.e. a medical condition, their travels, recipes they enjoy, etc...).

There are many website and blog hosting companies online to choose from. Many have affordable cost-effective rates and others actually offer free hosting. I personally have a "blogger" site (a blog hosted by the Google Company) and my domain registration (optional) is only $10.00 per year. I have incorporated Google Adsense into the site and readers can post comments on my articles, which I can personally moderate or delete as needed (i.e. spam posts or offensive ones). I do however feel it is important to determine the needs of your site, such as how many megabits and how much bandwidth a host offers through their websites.

You would also need to know how many pages you can add to your site (many offer unlimited space and pages).

The convenience of a blog is also in the fact that these will automatically archive each post you make, by month, day and year, so that as you post each new article, this is done for you. When seeking options on blogs or websites through hosting companies, doing an online search to read what is offered on these and comparing the costs of them can help one determine which type site would work best for them.

CHAPTER FOUR

My Plagiarism and Article Re-publishing Observations

(When Online Content is Stolen)

I recently posted the information following below, on an online forum that was not available to the public. The post was in regard to the subject of "plagiarism" (theft of intellectual property) and I feel the things I shared are worthy of being included as a chapter in this book.

My Post:

"When I was an editor for a thyroid health website, where I published 163 articles, I underwent training which included an extensive course on plagiarism. I wanted to share some thoughts on the subject that came from that course I took and from other sources I've learned facts on the subject from, over the past 8 years I've been publishing online.

First I want to express that I'm absolutely against plagiarism which amounts to theft of intellectual property.

At the same time, I've had experiences that made me realize the importance in being absolutely sure something I've published online has been plagiarized by someone else before making that accusation toward them.

One experience I had in this area was when after publishing two articles on the subject of thyroid cancer, for the thyroid health site previously mentioned, another editor for another topic on the site wrote a very similar set of two articles that had similar titles and similar outlines to mine. I was quite upset until closer reading of the articles and I realized they had more originality in them than I first recognized and the timing of their articles following mine only weeks later and the other basic similarities to mine was simply a fluke.

Even if this was not the case and their idea for these was sparked by my articles it still did not meet the definition of plagiarism. The experience made me re-examine myself for the possibility that I actually felt the other editor presented me some competition and that was actually where part of my concern was coming from.

My point being that if you feel you've been plagiarized, it is important to be specific if you plan to point it out to a party suspected of the plagiarism or others you may wish to involve in getting the issue resolved.

I've also previously wrote 70-plus articles for a "how-to" content site and have seen my outlines for these followed very closely by other how-to online properties. As far as republishing my own articles after having them on other sites, I have only done so from ones that allowed this and when I felt a need to do so as backup because some sites will not necessarily be around months or years from now.

I have also republished articles at times because sites I resigned from began a process of over-writing them when I left (replacing them, rather than deleting them) and a new editor would be stepping in. This occurred at the thyroid health site I describe above for example. I in-fact moved most of my thyroid subject articles over to my personal blog from that site for this reason and not solely for Adsense revenue purposes because republishing articles on more than one site can drop your Google rating as an author.

I have over 600 articles online to date, with only about 100 of them being republished from the thyroid health site.

I hope I'm never accused of plagiarism myself because for me personally, that would be somewhat of a slap in the face. I began search and research on health disorders (mostly the ones I am experiencing) in 2003 and have put more study hours behind this than some medical students have, who have become doctors (literally). I first began creating a website called "JimLow's Articles & Audios", in late 2004, where I published about 125 articles on thyroid, CFS, adrenal fatigue, anxiety, MVP, etc… I also moved those articles at one point upon canceling the site because I did not want to continue paying a hosting fee, when free hosting was available.

I did not place Google Adsense on that original site for two years because my purpose was writing and sharing knowledge with fellow health disorder patients and not to make money from the articles. I am now making revenue every way possible from my content because I realized over time, this does not diminish the benefit to readers of the articles and is a nice little benefit for me, the author and for the advertisers as well.

It would take a lot more time and effort for me to plagiarize than to write an article from scratch, drawing from my own knowledge. Do I write on subjects that have already been covered? Absolutely and so does everyone else with exception of the very first writers who originally covered subjects decades or 100s of years ago. Same subjects are covered endlessly online and if they weren't, we would have a very empty-looking internet.

Site administrations on most content sites have a feature in their software that searches for duplicate content before they accept submissions. If at some point, you feel your content has been stolen you can point-out your concern to them and ask them if they can run a duplicate content check for you.

The same thing can be done by pasting content from an article (titles and whole sentences) into a Google search, to see if it has been published by anyone else or use free online programs such as the Copyscape Plagiarism Checker."

Sites who Use Content without Permission

I have also experienced times of needing to ask
sites who posted my content without my
permission, to remove it. This is not the same as
plagiarism in which an article-publisher claims to
have written a piece that they actually extracted
in-part or in-full from someone else's authored
content. In this case it would actually come under
"copyright infringement" and "intellectual
property theft" definitions. One site I recently
contacted for committing this offense by
publishing my content in-full on their site without
permission was in regard to an article I wrote on
the subject of "invention marketing". The owners
of the website were in this line of work their
selves (consultation for inventors) and I found on
one of their pages, where they had pasted my
article-content. I wrote to them via their online
contact form and asked them to remove it
immediately. They were gracious and responded
immediately and offered to instead, simply
mention the article and post a link to it, which I
accepted as resolution to the issue.

This still gave them some benefit and for me as well, by helping to promote my article at the original link-source.

It is usually acceptable to quote small portions of content from another source, as long at it is only a snippet that's about 25 words in length and up to a maximum of 50 words. The author or source should be credited by name for the original article the quote is extracted from and a link to the content should be added. Most authors have no problem with someone quoting them, under these conditions and at the same time, the source quoting them is showing respect for their intellectual property.

CHAPTER FIVE

Tips on other Types of Publishing and Republishing

Formatting Books and E-books from Articles

Some content producers eventually compile articles they have written, into books and e-books. This can be done, as long as any articles one has published on content sites are not exclusive to them (all re-publishing rights turned over to them). Some content sites ask only for an exclusive on "digital rights" meaning anything online or down-loadable on electronic reading devices, such as e-books belongs to them. In this case an in-print book can still be published by the original author of them. Other content sites ask for an exclusive on articles for only a set amount of time, such as one year and afterward, the author can republish them, any way they wish.

Following, are tips on how to format articles into a format that can be published as a book or e-book: ---

One important early step is to look at other e-books and in-print books by reputable authors or publishers and use them as a guideline as far as book-structure goes. You'll note that a lot of them have the title and subtitle on the first page and possibly the author credit and copyright notation on the first page as well.

You'll notice that their next page might have a "dedication" (optional depending on type of book but can be added to any book) and in most cases is short – sometimes even just a sentence in length.

Afterward, a page for the "Table of Contents" listing chapter-titles can be added and then a page that gives an "Introduction" to your book (some books place table of contents after the intro and vice-versa). Each article you place in the book can serve as a chapter.

The next page after the Table of Contents can start "CHAPTER ONE" with the chapter's title in bold, in all large caps or underlined (different authors may do one or a combination of these). The content of the chapter would then be in regular print (no bold or all large caps words unless for highlighting).

With each new chapter/article, you simply do the same as I describe in the previous paragraph and at the end of the book you can add a "Conclusion" if you like but that-too is optional and depends on the type of book being published.

As far as indenting paragraphs, I use the double-space method, rather than indenting because I wrote for two very large content sites and their studies of site-visitors showed in regard to indentations versus double-spacing, that readers prefer double space paragraph separations (again other authors or publishers may disagree with using this method in books).

Also know that when you submit an e-book to most publishing platforms, they allow you to preview the file as it would look to a NOOK, Kindle or other e-book reader before you complete the publishing of it. If you see things not right in your word file, simply "save" your book submission information and don't publish until you've updated your file the way you want it to look and reload the book's content (word file) into the book file prompt when it is revised to your liking.

As far as page-numbering, Word.Doc files can be numbered – just look for the "Insert" prompt at the top of your word processor screen and select the type page numbering and at what page you want numbering to begin. What's nice about Microsoft Word page numbering is that the numbering will also appear if you convert your file to PDF (free conversion is offered online, via a Yahoo search).

This last part of advice will be more-so the advice some publishers may differ with me on but I have all of my own titles published on several large booksellers without professional editing applied to them. YES, pro-editing would improve them even more but with my having about 39 e-book titles and nearly as many books-in-print, it would be a massive expense for me to have this done in any way other than gradually, over time. In the mean-time, I wanted my information available out there, so published them at very near professionally edited level.

There are problems you'll have to deal with, including the fact that Word files will change to a different layout, when you covert them to PDF or EPUB but not always so significantly that it seriously affects the quality of your book.

Some publishers (fee-based ones) will try to convince you that publishing from Word.Doc files; even with conversions is a big no-no! – But, this is what I have done with all my books and I get great comments on them often from readers. In my case, with health-related titles, rather than novels, people are far more interested in my info, than in the professionally-detailed layout of my titles.

In-short, if you're publishing a novel, professional editing may be important but if your book is need-to-know information (i.e. How-To, Self-Education, etc…) a professional editor may be an expense that is not necessarily needed. I would however, run the content-file through word/grammar check and proof-reading of it to a willing listener/reader to make sure it flows as you would like.

Recording Audios for Publishing on Websites

Audios were something I enjoyed producing, for placing on content sites because I have personally always enjoyed informative information and books I could listen to via Mp3 downloads or on tape and CD.

I did find however, that audios do not receive as many clicks as do written works, so keep this in mind if you decide to submit audio content to revenue sharing websites.

There are software downloads available that allow you to simply plug your own audio player, into the back of your computer sound board and record audios that convert into Mp3 files that you can post on websites that are set up to accept them as content for use by site-visitors. What you need to accomplish this, is a player with an earphone jack (one that plays-back audio tapes and/or CDs) and a wire you can buy at a Radio Shack or other electronics stores with the standard-size male-jack on each end (the type seen on the end of earphones). You simply plug one end into the earphone input and the other into the "blue" input on the back of your computer tower's sound board. This blue input should be right next to the green input, where your computer speakers are plugged in.

The audio you play through the wire from the player, into the computer will have already been pre-recorded using a microphone, containing the audio you wish to make into an Mp3 file.

The computer recording software should allow you to hear what you are playing-recording, through your computer speakers. It should also have adjustable recording levels you click on to adjust, a choice of mono or stereo and other effects that might be needed. In fact you can also adjust the volume, by simply doing so from the player you are using.

Some of the audios I've posted on content websites are better than others. The reason for this is because it took me a while to find the better audio recording programs online and to know how to adjust the recording levels and other adjustments to make best-possible recordings. In reality, these different software providers make these programs easy to use and I should have experimented a bit more before posting as many audio downloads as I did so quickly on content sites. When I say "experiment", once you record a file, your own computer saves it in a file and you can click and play it back on your own media-player, to see how it sounds before publishing it.

To obtain software for downloading and recording audios, simply conduct a search on Google and use the search term "record tapes to CDs".

43

Following are the names of some I've used that can also be found via online search: "Blaze Audio", "Golden Records" and "Polderbits". When you find any of these, choose their "free download" option because this allows a free trial of them for about two weeks before you purchase the permanent versions.

I have always loved audios and they are wonderful method for sharing interesting information, stories, music and knowledge.

Some websites also allow video content to be posted by contributors, including that they have personally created or that they link-to from sources that feature videos and who allow links to them (i.e. YouTube).

Some sites also allow images to be posted as content by those who have rights to them, such as contributors who practice photography and have interesting images to offer for view by site-visitors. All of these types of content have potential to create page-views and/or clicks on ads provided to content sites by advertising firms.

In Conclusion:

It is my hope that the preceding chapters have offered sound advice to content producers who are seeking to benefit from websites who offer revenue opportunities. I would only add in closing that one should take the time to research the sites they are considering and to not make snap-decisions in choosing those for submitting content to. This demonstrates that one places real value on their intellectual works, plus it is simply good business to look out for one's own interest when entering into business relationships, online and otherwise.

(END - SECTION ONE)

SECTION TWO

How To Avoid Negative Online Publishing Experiences

Cautiously Marketing Your Intellectual Property

TABLE OF CONTENTS (SECTION TWO):

INTRODUCTION - SECTION TWO:

Approximately 7% of all retail sales occur online presently and business research firms predict that up to 210-billion dollars in total sales will be accomplished online for the year 2011 with an estimated 8% of total retail sales being predicted for 2012 or up to 250-billion dollars worth. Much of this business is in the area of published works, such as books and e-books being sold by reputable publishers including Amazon and Barnes & Noble and by reputable content websites that offer free public articles but who generate massive advertising income and retail sales (i.e. Associated Content Yahoo and About.com). Strangely enough, even with this type of growth in online business, there are still companies, large and small, and individuals who conduct electronic commerce, with a seeming lack of seriousness in regard to business ethics but with profit earnings as a high priority at the same time. It is almost as if they perceive long distance transactions as being something one does not have to conduct with the same ethics or moral standards as one would practice with interstate commerce that is conducted in-person or that requires some type of physical exchange.

In worse case scenarios, online businesses actually trifle with people or slight them and some actually cheat their customers or clients, as a regular practice. It's possible that they feel at more liberty to do so because of the fact that it is difficult at this point in time, to prosecute for illegal online transactions that occur or to even register complaints against some online businesses, who do not reveal their physical locations and who provide only a contact phone number but who reveal very little about their companies otherwise. While all computers have a unique IP address (Internet Protocol) and can be tracked by this and located by authorized legal officials, individual citizens cannot do so because such a practice can be considered illegal, when it is not authorized. Even large companies who do openly display their contact information can be difficult to investigate for dishonest online transactions, due to the fact that their electronic records can be manipulated and difficult to track.

There are ways however, that we as individuals who purchase from online business or who become involved with them in other ways (i.e. authoring content for publishers or websites) can call bad online business practices into question.

We can take action when we are affected by them, which can be done legally but with effective results. If we, who care about the future of electronic commerce, can begin to exercise our rights to be dealt-with honestly by online businesses, it can help to influence them, in a positive future direction. If we fail to do our part however, the internet, over time will begin to progressively cheapen in the area of content publishing and it will begin to become increasingly difficult to protect against unethical activity. This has already begun to occur on a wide scale but with some effort, we can begin to reverse this downward trend, while it is still possible to do so.

Within the chapters that follow, I will offer suggestions for helping to remedy experiences one might have with dishonest online entities or ones who fail to see reasonable interests required by those who enter into business arrangements with them and how to also avoid such experiences. I will cite several personal examples of questionable activities, practiced by online businesses I have dealt with, that negatively affected me, in the area of online publishing.

Certainly these same type practices occur in the area of retail sales as well and likely on an even larger scale but I feel my experiences, as well as my advice may help to provide ideas of how one can take a proactive stance in helping to effect positive change in electronic commerce of every type, including that which is conducted in the written content publishing field -- the marketing of intellectual property.

CHAPTER ONE

Avoiding Fly-By-Night Online Businesses

(A Simple Rule of Thumb)

As mentioned in the introduction of this section, there are online businesses, who reveal as little about their companies as possible. They may not have an "About Us" page at all or if they do include one on their website, it contains very little information about them. The more up-front type websites include lots of information about their companies, including a list of their founders and/or CEOs, the type of experience their staff has in regard to the business they are conducting and information about their office location (i.e. their physical address, phone number and email or fax lists).

When these type things are not included, this should raise a red flag to people who are browsing certain types of businesses online. Even when companies are new, one should feel far more comfortable dealing with them, if they reveal important information regarding their background and business operations, than when they are being elusive with this type information.

In some cases, unethical businesses avoid posting details about their companies because they want to be able to shut down their operations if needed, should they be pursued legally and leave very little trail behind them for being tracked down by authorities or investigating bureaus. These type companies are referred to as "fly-by-night" businesses, a term that has been around for a very long time and they certainly do exist online, although some may operate for many years before shutting down and reorganizing.

In regard to publishing companies for example, I looked into some of these for publishing my books and e-books, that were far less reputable than are the well-established ones but after careful investigation via online search, I decided that it would be a mistake to go with any of them. Much of my decision was also based on the fact that some of these publishers were fee-based print-on-demand (POD) companies and with the fact that even mainstream publishers, such as Amazon and Barnes & Noble, can publish e-books and books in-print on a POD basis, at no cost to the author/publisher, it would have been fallacy for me to have gone with these other publishers, on my low budget.

In addition to suggesting that one beware of online businesses that reveal little about their companies on their websites, I would also advise that it would be a good idea to conduct an online search of companies you are considering entering into business with, to see what their past clients are saying about them. This can be done simply by placing their name in the bar of a search engine. If a company has been in operation for any reasonable length of time, information will be found that is either positive or negative and possibly some of both, in which case one must balance the information found, best possible. While these suggestions may seem simple, they fall in line with the old saying, that "you can't judge a book by its cover". There are flashy, very technical looking websites that exist online, who are totally lacking in any proper business ethics and good business practices and one would do well to remember this fact.

CHAPTER TWO

The Better Business Bureau: Not Just a Slap on the Wrist

(Bringing Resolution to Bad Online Business Practices)

It is sometimes believed that turning a company or an individual conducting bad business, over to the Better Business Bureau (BBB) for mediation of a complaint, is ineffective and amounts to no more than simply a "slap on the wrist". This is not true however because unless they resolve complaints that are registered against them or they at least attempt to resolve them, they will remain on their BBB record as "UNRESOLVED" for three years. Many potential customers of businesses will look up their BBB complaint record, before doing business with them and this can be quickly accomplished online. If they find a large number of complaints or they see one or more complaints that have not been resolved within a reasonable period of time of them being registered, this is enough deterrent for many customers or clients to refrain from doing business with them.

BBB records can also be instrumental toward establishing the ongoing reputation of businesses.

In my approximate 8 years of dealing with publishing businesses, online, I have only had to resort to BBB complaints against two. The companies did however resolve these complaints quickly; one doing so within 48 hours and the other doing so within a week of my registering a complaint. It should be understood that some businesses who are BBB accredited, meaning they have membership with this mediating bureau, are sometimes given good ratings by the BBB, due to their promptness in attempting to resolve complaints registered against them. This is what the rating system is based on and it is not a rating of a company's business ethics in-general. Most people who do background checks on businesses, at the BBB website, are aware of this fact and so they also take into consideration, the number of complaints a company has against it and the nature of those complaints (i.e. contractual complaints or sales complaints, etc...). Also, if a business is BBB accredited, they are required to resolve complaints registered against them, within 30 days.

If a complaint is not initially resolved, they are then required to enter into mediation/arbitration with the complainer, to further attempt a resolution. The resulting status of "resolved" or "unresolved" is then, afterward displayed on their record for approximately 36 months.

The BBB has made it simple to fill out their online complaint form and by doing so; this places the complaint into the hands of the business in question, very quickly. Regardless of where a business may be located within the United States, a person complaining can register a complaint from the BBB office within their own state, since this would be the location from which they conducted their side of the business transaction resulting in a legitimately negative experience for them.

Businesses who are attempting to build an honest and ethical reputation, do not like seeing numerous complaints or unresolved complaints displayed publicly on their BBB record. For this reason, it can be an effective move on the part of a consumer or business associate, to register a BBB complaint when on the receiving end of dishonest or unethical business practices by online companies.

Certainly, if one has been cheated out of thousands of dollars or their intellectual property has been stolen from them, legal representation, involving an actual lawsuit should be pursued but for milder but concerning offenses, the BBB is often an effective choice of remedy.

CHAPTER THREE

My Heated Exchange with an Online Beatles Radio Station

(Putting the Blue Meanies in Their Proper Place)

I had a recent experience with getting into a tiff with a man who runs an online Beatles radio station website (I'm a lifetime fan of the rock group) and the fact that our correspondence evolved into a nasty exchange took me a bit by surprise. My problem involved my having sent them a PDF file of a book I had written, in consideration of being sold in their online store, which was a follow-up to my earlier email, asking if they were interested in reviewing the book, which they replied to in the affirmative. I simply requested conformation of their receipt of my intellectual property, within the submission I sent, which I had to request two additional times over a two month period because they would not respond. This was somewhat of a red flag to me because I had some authored works that were in-essence stolen from me previous to this, under very similar circumstances.

I was fortunately able to resolve the issue by complaint through the Better Business Bureau.

When the station owner did finally respond, he referred to my authored Beatles book titled *A Fan's Tribute to the Beatles* as "crap", in spite of not having read it and he called me a few choice names via email and ones that would actually fall under internet harassment laws in the US (his business is located in the UK). He resorted to this because he felt I had given his wife, who runs the radio station's corresponding Beatles memorabilia store a "difficult time" in my complaining about not receiving confirmation from them of receiving my book files by email attachment. He also said he was going to write a negative review for my book, place it online and send me a link to it once completed (Oh how vile thou art revenge!).

I had no idea the man would respond in this fashion simply because I expressed my disappointment in regard to his dropped communications with me, after I sent further information and PDF/Word files of the aforementioned book to him for consideration of distribution for it, through his online store (at his request).

I specifically asked that he please confirm receipt of the files and information I submitted to him because this gives me documentation when I send my authored material to someone via e-mail, especially to overseas locations. I also had to reformat the book because it had been converted into EPUB at one point for publication on the Google E-book Store and this was the only version I had saved (I now save both PDF and Word files of all of my books for backup). I had to re-separate all of the headings, re-do paragraph separations etc... for sending to the Beatles store and it took me most of a full day to do so.

I had no idea who ran the Beatles memorabilia store (this information was not included on their website), which was an extension of the radio station, in-fact I suspected it was pretty much a one man operation and that both the radio station and store were a one-man show (this was not far from correct). By no means was I purposefully intending to direct anything derogatory toward this man's wife, as was his accusation (she became the contact regarding my book submission to them). He was the person I was in contact with originally and I had no idea his wife even existed!

I suspected that the lady, who responded to my email regarding their lack of confirmation for receipt of my copyrighted materials, was either an employee of the radio station or someone using an online nickname (she signed her response with a first-name only). The station-owner uses a nickname, derived from the title of a Beatles song, rather than his real name and this is partly why I felt this woman was doing this as well. While I've listened to the radio station myself a number of times over the past few years, I had never once heard her name mentioned or the fact that the website owner even had a wife.

This entire episode started with my sending the PDF and Word files of my Beatle title book, which is a "fan's tribute", not a biography or a novel but simply a personal view of my love for Beatles music and my admiration for the men who wrote such beautiful songs. It is a short-length book (about 76 pages – no images). I do make mention of life-struggles these men have experienced as well as some Christian views I added-in, including my mention that John Lennon repeatedly apologized for his remarks regarding the popularity of the Beatles as compared to that of Jesus Christ, which he made in the year 1966.

I also mention John's period of seeking information on the Christian faith, including letters he wrote to Oral Roberts Ministries and donations he made to them at one time. My intention was to create a book that wasn't a typical "cutesie Beatles mop tops" repeat, with so many of these already being offered by booksellers. I actually wondered if something included in the book was offensive to the owners of the radio station but it turns out that their failure to confirm receipt of my submission was simply neglect on their part. With the fact that my intellectual property was involved, I simply had to follow through to protect my interests and their silence was logically very concerning to me.

When I originally wrote the man at the Beatles radio station asking if he might be interested in adding either the e-book or the in-print version to their online store product line, he replied within about two days. He stated in his email, requesting further information that the e-book version might be a good prospect for the store, with their recent adding of digital downloads to the site. I responded in telling him I would send PDF and Word files to him for review as mentioned previously.

Once a full month had past I asked once again, via a new email for confirmation that he received my files, but still no answer. Once yet another full month passed I sent an email expressing my disappointment that he didn't confirm my submission and that even a polite "no" answer would have sufficed, which obviously came across very offensive to him (my e-mail did not venture outside of professional etiquette).

His wife responded first to the email but I had no idea who she was and I actually suspected it to be the site owner pulling a prank, due to numerous misspellings and a lack of professionalism the response contained. My short response to them, that followed, should not have come across offensive but apparently it did (my request was good business and common protocol). I hold no animosity for this online Beatles radio station or toward the couple who run it however, when he informed me that a bad review of what he called my "crap book" was on its way to being posted online, I wanted to have my own rebuttal handy as well or what might be more properly categorized as "my side of the story", that I also planned to publish online if necessary.

He did not follow through with the vengeful, negative review and so I was not required to rebut any negative press from him either.

This is not actually the first time I have seen online correspondence turn sour, in-fact, some of the worst mud-slinging I have witnessed in my lifetime was on forums, message boards and even within article exchanges between authors at odds with each other. In my opinion, some of this is a form of venting anger and frustrations one has, toward those who are not actually responsible for their problems but that is being masked as anger toward the individuals it may be directed at. I personally try to avoid it, when I see hints of it being directed toward me by someone and in most cases when a person has sloughed me off, after I have gone to some effort to follow through on a mutually considered business prospect I simply walk away. In hindsight, that's what I wish I had done in this case involving the online Beatle radio station and despite the tiff that developed between us, I only wish them growing and ongoing success (sincerely). At the same time, it was my obligation to point out their lack of proper business protocol.

Hopefully, it will make them think twice before slighting someone else, who is following-through on a business proposal, that they-themselves have requested to be submitted to them.

The fact that business is being conducted online, rather than in-person, should not change its priority or the proper ethics with which it is conducted, especially with the fact that more companies, banks and other business institutions are now conducting transactions online, than at any previous time in our history and this trend continues to increase with each passing day. We, who are at the forefront of this growth, should determine to set a high standard of precedence for the future of online business and electronic commerce.

CHAPTER FOUR

Removing my Blog from a Major Revenue Sharing Website Conglomerate

(The Strange Practices of a High-Profile Content Farm)

I wish to mention at the beginning of this chapter, that the business practices of the website I will be mentioning following, are not in the "corrupt" or "dishonest" categories, nor are they necessarily unethical; they do however represent an over-emphasis of benefit for the website with an imbalanced lack of consideration for writers who contract with them, in my opinion (many former writers for them, share my view, while others view them very positively).

One reason I decided to write an article/chapter, actually naming a revenue-sharing content website is due to seeing many other writers specifically give their evaluations/revues of their experiences with Demand Studios, and so I thought I would add my own into the mix, for balance. Certainly this will not be an attack toward them however, I will be expressing some disagreement with their methods.

All of these I will mention, they consider to be under their editing and quality-of-content umbrella. Some readers might say that I'm killing any future chances I might have, to write for Demand Studios by publishing this and I would only respond in saying that I will never, at any point in the future, have any interest in writing for them. I will rather go my separate way, respectfully and wish them the best.

Approved for Rejection at DS

Some months ago, I submitted an application and a writing sample to Demand Studios (DS) and I was approved for a writing position. I noticed after approval, that they also have a blogger program, which sounded quit good (I publish a personal blog), although their description of the program was lacking in details. The program involves DS crawling your approved personal blog for new posts you have written and they will add those posts to the appropriate correlating DS website or they will add a headline to the blog-post on one or more of their sites. This increases their traffic and in turn, increases the blog owner's traffic as well.

67

The sparse information they provided regarding the program also mentions presenting bloggers with the opportunity to earn advertising revenue shares over time.

Ironically, they reviewed my health blog and accepted it as meeting their standards for being well-written and active, with a professional appearance that they are seeking. At the same time, I was writing my first three articles for them, under the writer program, which I was also accepted into. These articles were in need of being approved as well, in order for me to be able to write additional articles for them. One of my articles was approved and appears on their eHow website. The other two however, were rejected, which stopped my ability to submit additional content to them, as an approved writer.

Excuses...Excuses...

When I submitted those first three articles and was asked by their editors to make a few changes within a certain time limit, I was undergoing surgical biopsies that very week and was very distracted by it and also by awaiting results on the analysis, which were to check for nerve damage in my leg.

Some of the requests by the editor were reasonable, while some were a bit strange, with instructions for changes being written in such a way as to be difficult to understand.

My personal feeling is that the editor was in some way wanting to impress with technical language that did not make sense, rather than instructing with clarity. One friend I showed these edit requests to, who has far more knowledge than I in some areas of professional writing and from whom I have sought advice from on many occasions, stated that my instruction from the editor was badly in need of better explanation. Rather than request further ramblings from them however, I instead submitted enough changes that I felt would surely result in the articles being approved.

An Editor Scorned

The editor saw where I did not make a particular change they requested and when rejecting the articles they stated to the effect that I ignored one of their edit requests and their language made it evident that they were offended by this.

69

I will only add that some of what the editor referred to as not meeting guidelines, were in-essence, requesting that I not have any personal writing style included in the article. Some of the editor notes also stated that I was being too descriptive at certain points within the articles. This honestly makes me believe that some of the editors literally want instruction manual type articles that lack any personal touch to them. On the other hand this also likely depends on which editor is assigned over a writer's articles. I say this because I have since seen eHow articles with some personality from authors within them and many that do not at-all meet the type of standard this editor was seeking. Many eHow articles that can be found online, are very short in length as well, which I'm surprised does not send up a red flag to the search engines. I personally find it difficult to write an informative article that is also very short in length but this is obviously what the editors were requesting from me.

Rejected and Approved at the Same Time

Even with this having occurred, I kept my blog in the DS blogger program for several weeks following.

However, after a couple of months of observing what they do with one's blog I pulled mine out of the program. My reason for doing so is due to my perception of the program as being overly-beneficial for DS, with blog owners basically being avenues to further their conglomerate of websites. Amazingly, even with two of my three initially required articles being rejected by the editors at DS, they were accepting my blog posts for inclusion on some of their sites, such as eHow and LIVESTRONG.

The blogger program explanation on the DS site is simply too vague and I wrote them, asking questions for better clarification. Following below was my submitted message asking questions regarding the program, with their response to those questions, following below that.

My Questions to DS:

I have my blog in the blogger program and have some questions. I would greatly appreciate an answer to these, as they are not given detail on your pages describing the blogger program. - Thank You! ---

---

1. When my posts are picked up by a site such as LIVESTRONG or eHow, is the 1,000 page views calculation based on the "Headline Views" column or the "Post Views" Column, as posted in my Work Desk?

2. Is there a way to actually view the posts that are picked up from my blog and posted to one of the DS sites (links to these are not shown in my Work Desk)?

These questions are very important to me and answers to them, will help me to know how actively I will post on my blog (I may increase posts significantly but would like to know what is actually resulting from my blog activity).

Thanks again

The Reply from DS:

Hi Jim -

Thanks for emailing us!

When one of your posts' headlines is clicked-on from a publisher website, that's what we qualify as a "post view." ---

These post views are what you can generate revenue on. At the moment, headline views do not count towards the revenue share, as no ads are displayed along our headline widgets. From a quick glance at your account, it looks like you've got a few thousand headline views and a handful of post views.

As for viewing which posts are picked up, and links to them, we're about to roll out a new feature in the work desk that will display this info! We'll be in communication with the bloggers about that (it's been a popular request). We're thinking this will be finalized within 4 weeks or less.

Thanks for being in the network!

Best,

The DMS Team

It was nice of them to send me these answers however; there are still a few unanswered questions. If for example, one discontinues with the blogger program at some point (i.e. they die, become ill or discontinue their blog), do the posts added from their blog, to DS websites, remain their property from that point forward?

73

They do require at least one new post per week on your blog, to remain in the program, so if a blogger were to miss posting for a month for unforeseen reasons, does this mean kaput!? No, there's simply not enough to go on, to know whether or not the program will actually benefit the blog owner in the long run and so I removed my blog from the program. This is not a choice that comes from my rejected articles with their Writers Program or I would have done so much sooner. It is based on what appears to be strange practices by this online conglomerate (i.e. not already showing links to where blog posts are being added and a lack of explanation for what the program entails).

Achieving Traffic for DS

I wanted to add that the headline views they achieved for DS sites, with use of my blog for the approximate 3 weeks it was activated in their system, was "13,394" views. These were shown to be coming from Livestrong, eHow, Computer Shopper, Chicago Sun Times and Answerbag 2010. Correspondingly, post views during the same period were "17" and clicks to my blog were "1".

At this rate, within a year or so of posting on my blog weekly, I might have actually seen 1,000 post views, while DS would have likely received clicks in the 100s of 1,000s within the same time period.

Chasing Off Legitimate Writers

I also want to add that I previously wrote for another very high standard content site with strict editorship and I had 117 articles approved within less than a year of writing for them. I also received two editor's choice awards for articles there and an editor complimented article as well. While it's very unlikely that Demand Studios would admit this, in some cases, their editors are causing writers who are potential assets to their sites, to be chased off by them or to be wrongly rejected.

Of course there are writers who are happy there and I say more power to them if it brings them satisfaction and fulfillment. You will also have those who can brag about the big dollar pay-offs they have received however, this again has much to do with which editors they have been dealing with, especially in regard to their first three article submissions.

Some writers, including me, look at the whole spectrum of content writing, including being able to place a part of myself into my articles (personal style) and while earning revenue certainly holds major importance -- it is not the only consideration involved for many writers who are passionate about their written works.

Extreme guidelines are great if the only objective is revenue but some of us enjoy a little more freedom and this is actually partly the reason writers are referred to as "freelancers".

I have found by search online, where many formers writers for DS have made similar complaints to mine, plus many other types of disagreements being expressed regarding their practices.

In this case, I do not feel that DS is practicing dishonest business; they are however seemingly lacking respect for the personal writing styles of individual authors and they are not recognizing the apparent professionalism of others, whose work is being rejected by their editors.

They certainly have every right to operate their content websites in any way they wish but the negative press that has mounted against them and the high-potential authors who are staying clear of them as a result, is an effect that will either hinder their growth over time or they will remain unaffected and will continue to grow and to make an impact on the content revenue sharing website industry.

CHAPTER FIVE

A Content Site Who Deleted Contributor Articles with No Warning

(One More for My List of Negative Writing Experiences)

During my years as an author of online articles, which began in the year 2003, I have had both positive and negative experiences, producing content for websites. I recently contributed to a fairly well known content site, who suddenly deleted significant numbers of articles written for them by contract authors, for SEO reasons. The site I refer to will remain nameless, respectfully.

I recently became a contract member of this content website, where I was contributing to only one topic. The reason I was only writing for the one subject, was due to my feeling very wary of the website (a gut feeling I do not experience often). I will not attempt to say that this incident means that they haven't done good things for contributors but this particular event, I felt was not properly conducted by them.

It involved the sudden removal of many articles from their site that they felt were lowering their SEO ratings (Search Engine Optimization status). I was not the only member who did not receive an advance warning that our articles were being removed. In fact my email from them, explaining their decision for the content removal, came two days following my articles being removed when the topic they were posted under, was itself removed from their site (one that fell under religion and spirituality categories).

They did state on their forum following the action, that the removal was not based on quality of content (they practice strict editorial guidelines) and they were somewhat apologetic for removing it however, had some of the members, whose articles were removed, not backed up their work (saved to personal files), that would have been content gone forever for them. As you will see from my forum post below, which no longer appears at their site-forum, that the removal of content **was not** the issue but it was **the way in which it was done** that many of us, who were/are contract members of the website, disagreed with.

Like most people, I walked away from experiences like these and much worse ones, up until a few years ago when I decided that expressing opinions on these type issues publicly, helps us to learn from them. It can also actually help to change wrong policies in some cases and result in positive changes. It is my belief that wrongful activities can only grow, when people affected by them remain silent.

Following is the actual post I made, which was among many that other contributors also made in disagreement with the way in which our content was removed from the website:

My Post of Disagreement at the Content Site Forum (Since Removed by Me)

"In all likelihood, the administration will be deleting these posts but I for one will be saving mine and posting it elsewhere online. This website will of course find a way to smooth this over and anyone with administration will bend over backwards to defend what the site has done and may be doing soon. ---

In fact, writers who aren't on the receiving end of this type thing will often defend a site as well, even in the face of obvious bad practices. It's like the saying goes -- "Whichever side the bread is buttered on".

*I have an interesting story in this regard and I wanted to add it in this thread. First of all however, I want to mention that the less-quality content sites have resorted to this type thing from the beginning. I believe writers literally begin believing at some point that **all** content sites want to bless them but in reality, their own businesses-online properties always come first. That's not to say that some content sites do not partner with their faithful contributors, because many of them do but some of them are overly one-sided in their own favor and in this type business, there has to be a degree of both give and take. Some sites resort to underhanded things to increase their revenue, at the expense of those who literally make their business work and prosper.*

This is not the first sour event I've seen at a content site and I could give other examples. ---

I will instead cite only one that this event has similarity to (regarding the lack of notice given) and that also indicates in my opinion, that the site is actually going a similar direction. The site I refer to is a "How To" property, who after gaining 10s of 1,000s of articles from authors, suddenly decided to cut off revenue sharing. Many authors raised a stink over it and over the fact that the notice for it was very inadequate. In fact many of us who wrote for them, did not receive an email at all (I had them remove my articles afterward but it took some pressuring). I received no email regarding this event that has occurred at this website either, in-fact I posted a new article today before I realized this had occurred (also taken down).

I've been in publishing for a long time, including about 65 books and e-books. I've written for many content sites as well and I can tell you with no reservation that the removal of the articles by contributing members was not a SEO based problem. For one thing the bulk of the articles have not appeared long enough to determine them to be lowering the site's search ratings. ---

If you'll note, other sites have these categories that were removed from this site and they have never once reported them to be a ratings problem. Some of my articles in the category that were removed get more traffic than do some of my health titles at these other sites (same topic -- not same articles).

Who knows why the site has done this but I will tell you this -- if they can resort to a mass removal like this, they are also capable at some point of other such practices. Their agreement does state that they can make changes, cancel memberships, etc... for any reason and for no reason, should they choose. Trust me when I tell you that MANY content producers have been burned by this type of thing and it also often backfires on the websites.

What is the future of this website? Who knows for sure but whatever it might be, it certainly will not include me. If only I had listened to my inward promptings, I wouldn't have invested the hours I did, creating those articles that were removed (many of you spent far more time than I did writing yours). ---

*I did save them however and I hope others did the same, especially those who had many. The fact of writers not having the forethought to back up their work is one major reason notice should have been ample on this action. It's almost as if they wanted to sneak it past as quickly as possible. **It's not** necessarily the removing of the articles but **the way** in which they went about it -- very improper...period."*

My post above, no longer appears at the forum of the website in question. I hold no grudge against them whatsoever but I do hope that my protest and that of the other members there will result in their giving better notice to members, when this type of change is being made, involving their personally authored content. (Note: Content producers can be dishonest and can commit unethical practices as well.)

To repeat: This and any other negative experiences I have had, does not prevent me from recognizing that good, honest content sites exist, in-fact, the one I refer to above is not necessarily dishonest but this particular action on their part was improper from any standard.

It also caused distrust by members there -- a fact that some of them stated in their own forum posts at the site, following the event but hopefully something positive can be learned from it.

CONCLUSION:

It is my hope that the preceding chapters help to give online publishers and authors ideas on how to protest or to bring resolution to issues that arise regarding online businesses they enter into contract with, who do not treat them fairly or who actually resort to dishonest and/or unethical actions that affect them negatively. It is also my hope that those who are involved with online publishing see the importance in thoroughly evaluating any online business opportunities they may be considering. While negative experiences with electronic commerce can help one to learn valuable lessons, the best scenario would be to avoid them altogether whenever possible. This can often be accomplished by conducting online searches of companies and by observing how much information is revealed about them, on their own websites.

By taking these simple precautions, authors and self-publishers can increase their chances of entering into successful online publishing partnerships with reputable electronic commerce businesses.

(END - SECTION TWO)

SECTION THREE

Rants and Raves of an Indie eBook Publisher!

Achieving Success with Digital Books

TABLE OF CONTENTS (SECTION THREE):

INTRODUCTION - SECTION THREE:

Within the chapters that follow, I will offer tips to other indie/independent authors who are considering publishing their eBooks with sellers such as the Amazon KDP and Pubit! (Barnes & Noble) publishing platforms. I will additionally include some information regarding my personal experiences writing for content websites (sites that publish articles in exchange for ad-revenue shares), in consideration of the fact that many indie publishers begin their writing experience with these type venues before advancing onward to eBook publishing.

While I may at times have straightforward things to say about advantages or disadvantages involved in publishing and selling through these types of venues, I do not resort to degrading language toward those I have had less-than-positive experiences with. I will also be frank regarding sales or publishing issues I have experienced, as an independent author but since I do share much of this information from a personal perspective, there will be a few inevitable rants and raves added-in from time to time.

My best publishing experiences have been with the Amazon company, both their Kindle Direct Publishing (eBooks) and their CreateSpace (paperbacks) divisions. This doesn't mean that I don't have good things to say about other publishing platforms because I certainly do but the outcomes I experienced do not reflect what every independent publisher will experience with same venues or platforms. Many factors are involved in publishing success, including the genres one plans to cover (types and subjects of eBooks being published) and how one plans to promote them. At the same time, I feel there are things we can learn from fellow-publisher experiences.

If you're a publisher, especially of the indie type, I believe you will find my shared experiences to be interesting (some more than others but with each hopefully conveying a "lesson learned"). It is my hope that readers of this eBook, will glean a few helpful nuggets of information that will lend positively toward their own ongoing publishing experiences, including advice regarding cautions that should sometimes be taken when proceeding with the different types of venues that are available for developing authors.

CHAPTER ONE

Publish Your eBook Free on Amazon KDP

In this chapter-installment, I will start with a "rave" -- my own report of positive experience with the Amazon eBook publishing platform. I hope to convey the fact of how the platform offers ease-of-use, plus how it gives indie eBook publishers the advantage of having their works placed before a massive worldwide consumer audience and amazingly, it's completely free! I would like to also add at the front of this chapter, that I am not associated with the Amazon company, in any other fashion, other than being a very pleased user of their publishing/selling tools. Keep in mind that there are other free eBook publishing platforms available, including Barnes and Noble's "Pubit" program, which also offers ease-of-use for indie publishers and most authors will place at least some of their titles with multiple reputable sellers. I felt that offering a rundown of the steps needed to publish eBook works, will help those who are new to this venue or who have not yet published eBooks on their own (those who have previously used fee-based publishers only), a general idea of how a publishing platform works.

I will be using Amazon KDP as an example of a platform that is simple to use. An author actually only needs a completed eBook (formatted for reading by consumers) and also an attractive cover-image if possible, to place their work live on any eBook seller website, that offers a publishing platform.

I personally sell 100s of units between my eBook and book titles at Amazon each month, most of these being through KDP, which I began using in early year-2008 (it has never stopped growing and the numbers may someday reach into the 1,000s monthly). I love the fact that the platform also allows me to go into my eBook files and make revisions, such as corrections or adding more content to them, at any time following their original publication. I want to generally go through the steps for publishing eBooks on Amazon, via their free service, which was formerly called the "Digital Text Platform" and now called "Kindle Direct Publishing".

Obviously, before one can publish a written-work, it needs to contain interesting, enjoyable or helpful content and it needs to be formatted, so that it is of good quality and readability.

Spacing paragraphs, adding chapter-headings and including an introduction and table of contents, can all be important to adding quality and consumer-appeal to an eBook. Having a cover-image for it can also add appeal to it, especially one that is professional-looking in appearance or that is at least relatively close to a level of professionalism. If you do not have a cover for your eBook, Amazon KDP will provide a generic one (a "placeholder image" that looks quite good) but a personalized one is of course better when possible.

Independent publishers ("indies") have a great opportunity to have their works sold through Amazon via this eBook publishing platform and the mega visitor traffic their sites experience worldwide, is highly promoting for eBooks. You can register with KDP to publish eBooks, via this link: https://kdp.amazon.com/self-publishing/signin.

Once you are a registered member and you have a completed eBook you are wanting to publish with them, click on the "Add a New Title" button that appears near the top-page of your bookshelf (the publishing area of your account).

You then complete the following steps I have numbered from "1. to 14." shown below (it seems like a lot to complete but it is much easier than it appears and it becomes easier with each use of the tools they provide):

1. Click on the yellow "Add New Title" button near the top of your KDP Bookshelf page and then click in the "New Title 1" bar it will take you to on a new page (near the top again) and type in your eBook title.

2. Skip all the prompts below the title bar (unless the title is part of a book series, in which case you fill these in as directed) and then skip-down to the "Description" form and paste or type your eBook description-details into it.

3. Click on the "Add Contributors" button and when the spaces pop-up, add your name by typing it into the first and last name spaces and click the "Author" option in the drop-down menu (or other contributor ID option that applies) which further identifies you (there's also an optional "publisher" space and you can add your name again into that or skip it if you like).

4. The "Language" bar that indicates the language your eBook is written-in, should already say "English" in it, so leave it alone if that's the case or choose the correct language option in the drop-down menu.

5. In the "Publication Date" space, click on the miniature calendar beside it and click on "Today's Date" or choose/click another date within the month if you like.

6. Under "publishing Rights" click the little circle next to "this is not a public domain work", if this is the case (the "public domain" choice is for non-copyrighted works).

7. Click on the "Add Categories" button and choose up-to 2 of them from the drop-down menu (you may also have to click-on sub-categories that appear out beside the main ones, to better ID your eBook genres/categories). Also be sure to add your "keywords" in the bar provided for them (up to 7 are allowed and should be descriptive toward your eBook's subject-matter). The keywords are important in that they help your titles to be categorized better and to be more readily found by people doing search engine and Amazon site browsing.

8. Click the "Browse for Image" button and choose your eBook image from your computer (I usually use images that are between 1200 and 1285 pixels on each side) and after clicking the "upload" button, wait for it to say "upload successful" (the image may look unclear in the little window on the publishing platform page but will look clear on the Amazon website). The image tool will re-size your image as needed but if it is too far off from being a compatible size to be modified, it may warn you, that your image needs re-sized a bit and resubmitted (there are a number of free image resizing sites online for getting this done if needed).

9. Click the little circle that says "Enable Digital Rights Management" (unless you opt not to have them add this protection against people copying/pasting your work) -- it is optional. Your automatic copyright protects you from outright theft of your written work, regardless of the option you choose on this particular prompt.

10. Click the "Browse for Book" button and load your word.doc or PDF file, until it says "Download Successful". ---

You can then click the prompt to review your eBook if you like, which will appear in a reader on the page that looks similar to how it appears on Kindle devices (I love being able to review my submitted eBooks before finalizing publication of them).

11. Under the "Verify Publishing Territories" heading, click the little circle that chooses "Worldwide Rights - All Territories" (unless there are countries you wish to exclude via the other options that are shown within these prompts).

12. Under the heading "Please Select Royalty Option", choose the "70%" option, if your eBook is priced at between 2.99 and 9.99 (if it is higher or lower than this range, you'll have to choose the 35% option). These are the amounts of commissions/royalties you will make on unit sales of your eBooks and the amounts are calculated for you (to the exact dollars and cents), once you enter your retail price.

13. Under "List Price", you'll see a bar for typing-in your eBook's retail price, at the top of the squared-in area and after filling it in, you then click the little boxes beside each of the other countries that are listed. ---

This will automatically set the price for them as well, comparable to your listed-price first typed-in for the U.S. Amazon website (calculations are based on the value of U.S. currency, as compared to that of the other countries).

14. The last little square on the page that appears just above the "Save and Publish" button, needs to be clicked because it simply confirms your rights to publish the eBook and afterward, you either click the "Save and Publish" button or the "Save for Later" button (use the latter if you want to recheck things or make changes before the final publishing).NOTE: the little square prompt beside the "Kindle Book Lending" heading is already pre-clicked and is why we skipped this one (it cannot be un-clicked). NOTE: Amazon also offers a program called "KDP Select", in which borrowed eBooks also earn commissions for publishers. It is an optional program, which will be covered further in chapters that follow.

Another good thing about the KDP publishing platform, is the fact that if you overlook completing a step, it will tell you this, by highlighting the incomplete areas in red.

It will not allow you to publish your eBook, until you go back and complete them. Just like anything else, the process becomes more simple each time you use it and once you've published several eBooks, it becomes easy for you.

In adding a final note for this chapter, I will mention that if you use a publisher such as "Smashwords", which submits your eBook titles to multiple sellers including Amazon, this process is completed for you. The choice to use such a publisher is largely based on the amount of control an indie desires to have regarding the immediate monitoring of sales reports and exclusive self-promotion of published titles. I personally made the decision to publish my own eBook titles to each seller myself but as the saying goes "to each his own", some indies may prefer the option of having everything completed for them, regarding publishing and sales tracking.

CHAPTER TWO

The BooksOnBoard eBook Publishing Platform

During the final months of year 2011, I received an email from the BooksOnBoard bookseller website, inviting me to submit my eBook titles to them as an indie publisher. They stated in the invitation email that they were only inviting a small number of independents to participate in the new program and that I was one of them. I actually felt privileged to be one of the indies who were invited and I began submitting my titles immediately.

I submitted a total of 54 titles to their new publishing platform and within a couple of weeks, they placed 21 of these live on their website. They looked very nice on the site, in-fact, as nice as the book/eBook ads that the main booksellers were displaying. I also liked the browsing/search features of their site and I understood why they were the largest independent book selling company, existing online.

After my first 21 submitted eBooks were placed live, they had to take them back down temporarily, in order to edit something regarding the descriptions of them, having to do with the imprints, which needed to show the author as self-publishing them. They informed me about this change, by email.

While I awaited the republishing of them, I received a notice from Amazon as well, regarding their new "KPD Select" -- an eBook borrowing program, for Amazon consumers participating in it. For eBook publishers who enter their titles in this program exclusively for 90 day increments, a commission is paid on titles that are borrowed by consumers.

I decided to place nearly two-thirds of my own titles into KPD Select and before BooksOnBoard could republish mine, following their needed changes to the imprints on them, I emailed them, asking that they please not place any of them live again until I further notified them. This would give me time to determine which of my titles would still be available to other eBook sellers and not be exclusive to Amazon Select.

I eventually did notify them but their reply by email stated that many indies who originally submitted eBooks to them, did the same as I did, by afterward asking that theirs be removed, so that they could include them in participation with KPD Select. They stated in the email, that they had obtained the services of a secondary company to operate the publishing platform and that the adding, followed by removal of many titles originally submitted by indie publishers, had proven to be expensive and that they were suspending the publishing platform for independents and would only be doing business with established publishing companies, until further notice.

I appreciated their notification to me, describing their reasons and while I sincerely felt regret for having participated in causing this problem for them, I also knew that my participation in the new Amazon program was a necessary move for me. At the same time this occurred, I was having ongoing problems with several other booksellers, while my Amazon experience was very solid and this continues to be the case.

In-short, I have never been treated better as an indie publisher but this does not mean that I don't see great merit in some of the other booksellers out there, who may very well begin to create more success for indies over time. As they do, I will have the same commitment and appreciation for them, in keeping my titles on their websites.

I still believe that I will always have a certain percent of my titles enlisted in KPD Select, for as long as it continues to be available (hopefully permanently) but this will still leave lots of them available for republishing with the other booksellers who remain solid with sales reporting and eBook/book search capabilities on their websites. I do hope that BooksOnBoard reopens the eBook publishing platform because they appear to be a solid company with great growth-potential for independents. Should they again invite more indie publishers to participate in a publishing platform again, in the future, I will be try to be one of the first in line, to resubmit my non-exclusive titles to them, if I am accepted. They are a quality bookseller and I would welcome the opportunity.

I added the preceding information in this chapter, to demonstrate the fact that competition between booksellers, can sometimes result in these types of scenarios taking place and in fact companies have been known to literally dissolve as a result of fierce competition that causes them massive loss in market shares. I personally hope to see several major booksellers to continue their availability to indie publishers because this helps us to avoid having all of our eggs in one basket so-to-speak and helps us to experience the ongoing expansion of our titles that we are seeking.

CHAPTER THREE

Mean-Spirited Spam Book and eBook Reviews

As an author of eBooks and paperbacks, I occasionally see book reviews appear on my works, at seller websites like Amazon and Barnes and Noble. I will now add somewhat of a "rant" regarding negative reviews in this chapter.

Spam Reviews

Most reviews I see posted for my published titles, are at least moderately favorable toward my authored works and some are very positive but ever so often, I will see one appear that is flat-out mean-spirited or those that actually amount to spam reviews. I have only actually flagged one of these negative types in all of the time I have been publishing on bookseller's websites (since 2008) and the reason I did-so in that case was due to the review-poster literally slamming a book I have available on the subject of Chronic Fatigue Syndrome and Fibromyalgia, in order for them to also recommend another author's book that they stated was "better than all other books available on the subject put together".

Amazingly, the bookseller whose site the spam review appears on, for some reason did not detect the review as containing spam and yet by even the strictest definition, that is exactly what it amounted to.

Booksellers Should Screen Mean-Spirited Reviews

The review poster actually included the wording to the effect that my eBook on the subject was "a rip-off" and they actually titled the review to the effect of "don't waste your money". I was amazed that the bookseller allowed the review to be posted and I am monitoring it to see if they will remove it, after my having flagged it. I will also mention that the reviewer claimed that the eBook was "too short" and yet it contains 12 chapters and over 9,000 words, at a price of only $2.99. I have fellow-publisher friends who I exchange book reviews with on-occasion and one of them has already posted a favorable review for the same eBook, after I provided them a free copy for adding their own review, in order to help offset the negative one (I recommend this method when unfairly negative reviews appear on titles deserving better reader-comments).

The better review that was added behind the spam one, mentioned the fact that one of the chapters contained in my eBook title, was awarded an "editor's choice award" in 2009, when it was previously published by a reputable content website. This will help to offset the attack-review should the bookseller for some reason, not remove it (at the time of this writing, it has remained for several months).

Illegitimate and Unethical Reasons for Negative Book Reviews

Why do people write extremely unkind reviews that obviously are not merited by a published work? In some cases, these are actually posted by real readers who are simply venting their frustrations toward books they have read that did not meet a standard of perfection they were seeking or that did not solve a problem for them as well as they had hoped. I know for a fact that other authors experience the spam and overly-negative book review scenario because I have been told this by them, firsthand. In some cases, reviewers may resent the fact that an author was able to publish a book on a subject that they failed to accomplish written works on their selves.

They may in some cases, have their own authored work available and they feel they can direct more attention toward it by degrading work published by other authors, on the same genre or subject. Some readers of this article-post might actually ask at this point, if I really believe this type of scenario takes place and I would respond by saying that **I certainly do**. In some cases, these type reviews are posted by fans of other writers or by friends of them, which would be far more acceptable, if it is a positive review for their own titles, rather than unfair negative reviews for titles by authors that they feel are competing with them.

Another reason I know for a fact that overly-negative and spam reviews result from the type scenarios I describe above, is due to my having been informed about this by writers-groups who enter into arrangements for exchanging positive reviews with each other. I have so-far only exchanged reviews with two authors, on less than a dozen of my approximate 70 published titles because I prefer to see them posted by readers, who are simply consumers but I do have these fellow authors on standby, to review any titles I see attack-reviews appear on.

This is so that they can offset them by posting a counter-review with more positive language included in it. I always tell them to rate the book honestly and to not include any biased favoritism in it (this would not be doing the author a favor).

Red Flags

The fact is that booksellers will not publish works that are obviously poor-quality or that are lacking enough content in them. Of course there are titles published by authors that are not deserving of praise or that do deserve a degree of criticism however, when reviews are overboard in the negative direction or include attack language or literally tell consumers to not buy a title, this should raise red flags with booksellers.

As previously mentioned, these type reviews can simply be posted by consumers who are venting frustrations because a book was not as life-changing as they had hoped it to be or they may be posted by authors or friends/fans of authors who are hoping to curve any competition they feel competing titles may present them.

108

I will also mention that the same seller who allowed the overboard review for one of my titles, that I describe above, also recently allowed another highly-negative review on another eBook I have published on their site and in this case I honestly believe the reviewer did not purchase the title. I believe this due to my having the title unpublished for a period of time and I had not sold a copy of it on the seller's site for a number of months. The review appeared in February of this year (2012) and yet the bookseller did not sell a single copy of the eBook during that month or for five months previous. This makes the review <u>highly suspicious</u>.

Of course a book-title might simply be legitimately bad but if this is the case, why would a bookseller allow such a title to be published in the first place or to continue being offered for sell? No, in most cases, overly-negative or attacking reviews that sometimes contain spam language, are simply not legitimate and authors should be prepared to report these or to offset the negative effects of them by soliciting additional reviews from ethical readers of their titles.

CHAPTER FOUR

Amazon's KDP Select: A Sales Boom for Me!

During the December month of year-2011, I decided to place a significant number of my eBook titles into "Amazon KDP Select" - a promotional commission-paying, eBook borrowing program that requires exclusivity of titles you place into it (for 90 days at a time). I had less than half of the month of December left when I placed mine there and I saw about a dozen borrows of various titles right off the bat! Now that January has almost swung-past (at the time of this writing) my number of borrows has already reached "21" in number. I feel however, that part of the promotional power of the program is the notation on your titles on Amazon, showing them to be available for borrow by KDP Select members, which in-itself promotes both borrows and sales of them. It adds just that bit more of interest for consumers to check into the titles further when they see this notation added to them. The reason I believe the program promotes both sales and borrows is due to the fact that my sales through Amazon in-general have spiked, since placing them there.

I will admit that I'm proud of how my sales and promotion for my titles has evolved on Amazon. They have simply done very well by me and I'm as pleased as can be, to be a part of this vastly-growing company, as an indie publisher. Some publishers, both indie and companies, might see sales numbers like mine (in the 100s per month) and find them to be low in-comparison to their novels and romance titles, that have massive outside promotions for them however, my title-sales (mine being mostly health disorder subjects) are seeing steady growth at Amazon and for an indie with limited promotional power, I feel my numbers are quite good.

The increase I'm seeing through KDP Select is significant and I'm anxious to see what coming months/years will reveal sales-wise. As I have stated in past online articles, my love of writing is not based on profits from sales, although I certainly enjoy that aspect but it is also my love for sharing information I believe will be helpful or inspirational to others. So when my numbers go up, much of my enjoyment and pleasure from writing, is knowing I have reached more readers.

Are there both pros and cons to placing eBook titles into a program like KDP Select? It actually kind-of depends on how you look at it but the short answer is "yes, there are both pros and cons". I've already described the pro aspects, from my perspective/experience, so now I'll mention a couple of the drawbacks. First, "exclusivity" places all your eggs into one basket so-to-speak, if you enter every title you have into this type program. A publisher might instead place only their select or prime titles into exclusivity and leave others on different seller-sites. The other drawback is that sellers you might remove titles from, to place into this type program, might feel a bit slighted for you having done so.

When I made the decision to place most of mine into the program, I removed them from the BooksOnBoard seller, among others however, they had already taken my titles down from their site to make a change to the imprints on them as mentioned in a previous chapter, so I caught them at the point before they reapplied them to their website. I actually told them to hold-off on republishing them and I added that I hoped I was not "burning a bridge with them".

Once I knew which of my titles I would not be placing into KDP Select, I wrote BooksOnBoard again and listed the titles I wanted to publish with them. They eventually wrote me back, stating that they were discontinuing the program for indie eBook publishers, at least for a period of time, due to many of them switching many of their titles to KDP Select exclusivity, as I did.

Sellers should be open to publishers protecting their interests, in this type situation because they would do exactly the same thing for their own businesses if a similar opportunity had arisen for them. I can absolutely be solid and faithful to a seller who does me right and who I'm doing right and I will openly praise them but "business is business" and sometimes difficult decisions have to be made.

When I make changes that aren't always in the interest of someone else I might be in arrangement with, I always do-so respectfully and always without burning bridges if at-all possible. Beyond this, I'm not sure what else a person can do, when they are protecting the interests of their life's work.

I spent literally 1,000s of hours over an 8 year
period writing my works and they are very
important to me.

There's always that possibility that a program like
KDP Select will fizzle-out over time and my
belief is that this is why they only require 90 day
exclusive increments on publisher's eBook titles
but right now, the program looks like it might be a
growing and ongoing success for sales and
promotions of eBooks -- and for me, it has
literally started with a boom.

CHAPTER FIVE

Is it a Good Thing to Write for Content Websites?

I mentioned in my introduction, that I would be relating some experiences I have had with publishing articles on content websites, which is something I did for several years before I entered the eBook and paperback book publishing venues. In this chapter, I will be relating my past experience writing for a particular site, that is one of the more reputable ones in their field.

Let me also immediately say at the start of this chapter, that I personally have no reason to believe the company has committed anything unethical or dishonest. I can say that they are extremely business-protective-oriented (a logical attitude to the proper extent).

Writers who contract with content websites like the one I will be referring to, are literally the "life-blood of their companies" and who have brought them to their past and present growth-status.

This could not have happened for them without quality content from authors and these sites would not exist today without the vast flow of articles being submitted to them.

The Removal of 50,000 Articles

From July 2009 to February 2010, I authored 117 articles that were carried live by this website and after they removed approximately 50,000 articles, at the start of year-2012 (yes, that's right -- *fifty thousand*), in order to improve their website-ratings, this still left 91 of my articles on the site (they removed 26 of mine). They informed their writers, about the article removal, via their account pages, rather than by email (at least I never received an emailed notice) and within their explanation, they stated clearly that the removal of the content was not a reflection of the quality of the writers but was rather due to them implementing much stricter editorial guidelines. They also stated that in some cases of articles being carried by them, it was their selection process "getting it wrong" -- the implication being that their editors should not have approved these articles in the first place.

Some websites, have also cited the new enforced website guidelines called "PANDA" and "Farmer" (required updates), that brings rating penalties against websites that fail to adhere to them, as a major reason for their decline in success and readership growth.

Why I Resigned as a Writer for the Content Website

In 2010, when I resigned as a writer from the website, it was due to my ongoing problems with editing changes/requests. This had nothing to do with their asking me to make changes to articles I submitted (I always did-so immediately upon request) but it rather had to do with liberties one editor in-particular, was taking, by making major changes to some of my articles, without rather asking me to make them myself (administration seemingly did not recognize the seriousness of the problem, involving a writer's copyright). My experience in no way, reflects the practices of the site in general and the lack of attention to the problem, may have been due to ms-communications that occurred within the site-administration.

I felt a need to mention this because I also dealt with a number of great people there, in spite of my negative experience in regard to the particular editor I refer to.

I will admit that I would not have agreed to some of the requests made by this editor, had I been asked to make them myself but it was blatantly wrong for them to make some of these changes, without my prior agreement to allow them. Small obviously-needed changes by an editor were certainly fine with me, in giving them liberty to make them (i.e. overlooked misspellings, small changes to improper structure or punctuation mistakes) but changing the meaning of the content itself was unacceptable to me. If I refused any requested changes required beyond these simple types, they could have then simply denied publication of the article in question. I would have then published the rejected-article on another website or on my personal blog.

To be more specific regarding this issue; I began submitting articles under the "religion" category -- specifically ones for the "Christian" section of the website. I believe this specific category has since been eliminated from their sites.

118

Several of these still appeared live there in the later months of year-2012 and a number of these were on the subject of Bible prophecy. The editor, who has since been promoted to a senior editor position, was apparently a bit biased toward psychic phenomenon and in places within articles, where I used the word "prophecy", she replaced it with the word "predictions". The biblical word "prophecy" is considered absolute by Christians while the psychic word "prediction" implies "a percent of probability or failure" for a foreseen event to transpire. I explained this to the editor and let her know that I could not allow the word-changes to remain and so I changed them back to the proper words and she afterward, dropped that particular requirement.

The same editor also began to re-write sentences and sometimes entire paragraphs within my Christian topic articles, so that they had more of a psychic or spiritism/mysticism flavor to them (for lack of better terms). She also began to argue with me regarding the interpretation of certain Bible passages I was writing on, at which point I complained to the site administration.

Advice and Cautions for Independent Publishing Authors

To make it clear, let me mention that the interpretational remarks I made within articles, were those of general agreement within a large percent of the fundamental Christian community and I know this to be a fact, due to my being in Christian ministry and evangelism for nearly 20 years (1983 to 2001) and graduating theological studies with Liberty University in 1996. The debate this editor engaged in with me, actually became a bit bizarre because once I would explain why I took the position I did with a biblical doctrine, she would bring up another aspect to argue with me about (I joined the Christian topic to write and **not to debate biblical interpretations**).

I Received a Reprimand for My Complaint

The site administration who became aware of my complaint, immediately defended the editor in question. They praised her highly and stated that they felt it was improper for me to have made a complaint (my email was filed in a business-like manner and my disagreement contained no disrespectful language toward the editor).

They made me feel as if it was improper for me to have contacted them regarding the issue and yet my disagreement addressed directly to the editor was not taken seriously by her and the issues <u>were not</u> resolved.

I knew her disagreements with my articles, which were actually based on "meaning" rather than "editing" aspects, would have continued to be written by me, under the heading that I wanted to submit many more articles under (my goal was to eventually have 1,000 articles live on their site -- with many new health titles also planned).

At this point, I took my issue to their writers-forum and posted about it there because I knew I was leaving/resigning as a writer and I felt the issue was important for the sake of future writers and that proper attention was not given to it, in spite of the obvious infringing nature of it.

I was also reprimanded for posting as a member on the private forum about the issue but my resorting to the posting, was due to failure for resolution via email communications.

Other Issues at the Content Website

Another issue that I felt was causing some difficulty at the content website, was their announcing frequent "writing challenges", such as "30 articles in 30 days" (plus many other variations of push for increased content), meaning if writers completed this many articles, within a given time-frame, they would be listed among the achievers on the website, via a recognition page. This seemed like a push to increase the numbers of content for the site, quickly and yet they wanted articles to meet a strict guideline for quality (an obvious conflict between quality and the number of content-pieces being coerced from writers). It was likely during these times, that editors became overwhelmed and had no choice but to approve articles coming to them for editing, in huge numbers. These may very well include some of the articles they have recently removed from the site in huge numbers.

When I began writing for them over two years ago, there were times I saw "PV (3 months)" at over 61,000 and I saw my revenue per month at over $100.00 at times and fluctuating between $50.00 and $75.00 for a number of months.

As of January, of 2012 my "PV (3 months)" was 7,554 and my revenue split was running at an average of about $10.00 for 3 or 4 months. Profit has never been my only reason for writing as previously mentioned and for the first two years I wrote articles online in-general, I wanted nothing in return for them but readership. When it comes to a website that enforces very strict editing guidelines, writers are certainly worth a split of the profit they are making for these content, revenue-sharing venues. It's possible that their cutting back of 50,000 articles that were under-par, will help them to gain back a higher rating and market share (only time will tell). **I sincerely do not wish them ill** and I actually hope the downturn recovers for them.

I wrote to them a few times over the past several months, to see if I would receive a response but they would not reply to me, in spite of my sending messages to several people within their administration. I tested this further, by sending request to be reinstated as a writer but still no response from anyone. The last time I wrote them (January 2012), I asked that my remaining 91 articles be removed from their site -- still no response from them of any kind.

What Does the Future Hold for Content Sites?

Another website I wrote-for, during a short time period, early last year (2011) actually did the same thing, in attempt to recover from a downturn in site popularity by removing 1,000s of slightly less quality articles (I removed my own remaining ones at that point). In the case of this content property, the cutback of articles <u>did not</u> improve the site's status according to a recent article in "The Freelancer Today" online magazine and they have discontinued writing availability to non-professionals and are now only working with a very few select writers. All other freelance writers were given notice of discontinued revenue share and writing access, as of December 15, 2012. The same article that reported the failure of this other content website, which also reported on a major downturn in popularity for the "Life123" content website, posed the question as to whether this same future might be in store for other highly successful content websites such as "Demand Studios", which is reported by some sources, to now be the largest freelance, revenue-sharing content website on the market today.

124

I would ask this same question regarding the content site my articles still appear on. -- Will they follow the same downward trend or will they recover? Current writers for them will simply have to wait and see. As for the question posed by this chapter's title, as to whether or not content websites are a good thing to write for, I would answer by saying that under the right circumstances and conditions, which likely varies between each writer and each website, they are potentially a very good venue write for. I do suggest that writers are careful to read the terms and contracts offered by them and to make sure these allow for them to remove their articles if necessary, free-and-clear of any retained rights to the content by the website, so that they can move them to better publishing venues. (More on the content websites subject in CHAPTER SEVEN)

CHAPTER SIX

My Recent Bizarre Experience on a Publishers Help Board

With this being an eBook in which I am relating personal experiences, I wanted to add a chapter in regard to an experience I had recently at a forum for publishers of eBooks, provided by a major bookseller (not associated with an Amazon company). Please note that this article is not intended to imply that the forum I refer to, is not a helpful place of information exchange for publishers because I believe it is and let it also be understood that bad experiences on forums can potentially happen on any of them regardless of their purpose and quality.

Why I'm Relating this Experience

I have several reasons for wanting to relate this experience, the main one being the fact that forum-posting is a form of online publishing. I also want this article-post to offer some warning regarding forum involvement in general.

Forums and message boards can be <u>wonderful things</u> when they are moderated correctly but those that have inadequate moderation (very sparse, imbalanced or near non-existent) can become more of a hindrance than a help for users. I do not place the Publishers Help Board I describe in this chapter, into the negative category because I believe it to be a **largely helpful forum**. I will add however, that the experience I had there (described below), though likely rare, demonstrates the fact that one should proceed with forum activity, with reasonable caution. One importance in the need for caution, comes from the fact that negative exchanges are indexed online, indefinitely and can be viewed by readers who see these types of posts that are connected to the authors, who also have eBook titles for sale (many use their titles in their forum signatures and profile bylines).

Let me also mention before I begin relating the experience I had at the forum, that this is only one of dozens of times I have either experienced similar scenarios at forums or have seen them occur to other members of them.

In at least one case, I actually saw a forum taken offline as a result of negative postings (attack and harassment posts), with the majority of its posts being taken out of index by search engines as well. In the past, I served as a moderator at several forums and my own combined posts at these approached approximately 5,000 in number. I became experienced enough at spotting negative behaviors at them, to know when it was evolving into harassment or attacks between members.

A Worse Case Scenario for Non-Moderated Forms

On one other forum I will mention, at a very popular content website, the "Religion & Spirituality" forum, evolved into a place of continual religious bigotry that was as vile as it can become, with every possible foul word, including the "f-word" being directed at members. I not only discontinued any involvement in the site-forum but I removed approximately 275 articles I had on the correlating content website, due to their administration not removing the offensive posts and being absent in regard to moderation (I cover this experience in another of my book/ebook titles).

Even non-moderated forums require intervention by their providers if things get out of hand on them.

My Publisher Help Board Incident

Now on to my forum experience (Please again understand that this does not reflect the standard of the forum in-general and I'm relating this experience due to it being associated with a "publishing" platform.):

Approximately 15 months ago at the time of this writing, I joined this Help Board, to communicate with fellow-publishers. My total number of posts over the 15 months was "127" (105 of these were replies), many of these were on the subject of formatting and other ebook-publishing related topics. Admittedly, of the 22 thread-topics I started personally, many were in regard to "sales reporting issues" that were occurring with the associated eBook publishing platform (sales being delayed in being applied to publisher's reports) and some of these threads were follow-up ones, in-which I would report a problem being fixed.

Some of my posts, all of which averaged less than 8 per month, would not have continued on the subject, except for the fact that the problem with sales reporting <u>continued</u>. The site administration actually informed publishers that the problem was occurring, both by emails to us and by occasional forum updates.

In spite of this fact, there were times it took them several weeks to become informed about the issue as it would recur (a fact confirmed by them thanking publishers on the forum, for making them aware of it).

The Bizarre Attack Posts

At one point, one of the forum members launched an attack toward me, complaining that I was posting too-frequently regarding the ongoing problem with sales reports and related issues (they are still fixing related problems, even as I write this chapter) and I was taken-back by this fact because first of all, it was for the benefit of all publishers that the problem continued to be pointed out by members, for resolution to occur.

I was literally advised by a man with this site's Business office, a year previous to this, whom I spoke to by phone, that their administration needed "frequent and straightforward communication" or they might not respond or investigate complaints, due to them being overwhelmed with emails. He literally stated to me that "you have to shout at them to get their attention" (a verbatim quote). After about 15 months of their eBook publishing platform being in business, they are now starting to put significant fixes on the issues publishers have been experiencing/reporting since its launch in late September, 2010 (I have 24 ebook-titles that continue to be listed there) but this has required diligence on our part.

Why Attack When you can Ignore?

The forum member who attacked me for my part on the forum, in attempting to get the needed attention on the sales reporting issues, should have simply avoided those threads however, since another member at the forum PM'd me (personal message), stating that they-too had been attacked by this individual, I knew his complaint regarding my posts **was not legitimate**.

Whatever his true problems are they are not
actually caused by the posts of forum members
(there is something deeper involved).
Coincidentally, this member would post regarding
the fact that he had eBooks published on the
associated platform but he refused to list the
names of any of his titles. This allowed him to
post attack-threads without readers of them
connecting his forum behavior to his published
titles, which as a result, could potentially affect
consumer perception of his character in general
(something he was obviously avoiding).

The problem with this scenario, is the fact that
people can potentially pose as authors by joining
a forum, but who in-reality have not published
any titles. In some cases, they join forums in
order to market services of some type -- which is
something this member was also doing (he was
making an eBook formatting service available and
using the forum to advertise it). The best solution
to this possibility in my opinion, is for the forum-
administration to require new members to list at
least one of their titles on their forum signatures,
to confirm their status as legitimate authors.

Strangely, this member posted in a thread, claiming I had posted on the subject in-question (problems with sales tracking/reporting), "4,398,743 times", which of course was meant for sarcasm. I posted a thread to correct this claim and included no attack language within it whatsoever but I did address it <u>directly</u> to this member and an Administrator/Moderator censored (removed) my corrective post (it was likely flagged by the other member who could apparently dish-out harassment but who could not withstand correction for it).

His posts however, which did include attack language and harassment within them have been allowed to remain on the forum (due to my not flagging any of his). My feeling is that the moderator could not investigate the problem as well as it should have been, possibly due to time constraints. The option to "ignore" the posts on my part was hindered by the fact they were directed at me and were not ones I saw between other members that I could have easily bypassed.

I actually sent this member who started the negative exchange, an apology PM to him.

This is the response I received back from him, shown in italics below (I PM'd him a total of "4" times -- 2 of them attempts at apologies):

His Reply:

"You have some serious issues if you're still crying over something some random stranger said to you on the internet weeks ago (.

Let me explain it a different way - STOP MESSAGING ME. I have no desire to hear from you, I don't care about anything you have to say, be it an apology or whatever. Geezus I feel bad for any chick that ever tried to break up with you because if it's this hard for me to get rid of you, being a complete stranger, my guess is you stalked ex's for years.

G O A W A Y"
(Note: This reply I received following my apology-attempt, was an attempt to reverse the scenario -- to claim I was pursuing an argument and that I was the one on the attack or who has "serious issues". Also: While I relate this experience, I do not hold a grudge against this man but sincerely wish him recovery from whatever his problem may actually be.)

When Legitimate Business Threads are Hijacked

This is the attitude of the individual who was not moderated on the forum (in italics above) and as a corrective point, it <u>was not</u> a "random something" he directed at me but rather a series of posts he addressed me with, in several threads. This is the reason I no longer participate in posting on that forum (respectfully). I felt that business threads, literally having to do with publisher's livelihoods, should not have been hijacked and degraded by this individual, who may or may not actually be an author.

In reflecting back to what the associated website employee advised me by phone (to be persistent), he also told me that a common complaint of publishers was "no reply to emails" and that they needed to put attention-getting headers on them and to send them repeatedly if-needed, to solicit a response.

This is basically what some of us were doing through the provided venue of the "Publishers Help Board", as an alternative to overwhelming them with emails.

My Concluding Advice Regarding Publisher Forums

If a person who joins a forum, finds that they can't resist the urge to attack other members, my suggestion would be to read other's posts as it helps but **not to post**. Also, when someone who is a posting member reacts with disagreement to a thread that is offensive to them or one that is posted for the purpose of attack or harassment, they should bypass those threads and not read them (very simple). It's the same principle one uses when they watch television but they are not interested in what they see on certain channels -- just change to a different one!

If you cannot help but see something on a publicly-displayed TV station that literally goes out-of-bounds and should rather be restricted to certain age-groups or that should not be on the air at-all due to bigotry or other issues, simply contact the cable company, the network or satellite provider, just as you would contact the moderator or administration of a website that provides a forum. It may or may not help but we do our best to keep these venues from degrading and remain helpful for those they are intended for.

Believe it or not, there are actually social forums designed for attack posts, "contests of wits" or that are sexually explicit, etc... If a forum is not of these types but is designed to help people but begins to degrade due to lack of moderation and legitimate members do not attempt to do something about it, this can contribute to a negative direction for publisher-forums in general.

Online forums have genuine potential that can be both positive and negative but much of this depends on proper administration to moderate/remove potentially negative posts and threads.

CHAPTER SEVEN

Content Farms: Authors Beware!

Content websites glean articles from writers/authors who are looking to publish their works online. There are literally 1,000s of these type of sites that are now often referred-to as "content farms". Some sites might see this term as being derogatory however, in many cases, this term describes these types of writing venues correctly because they are in-essence planting seeds of advertisement toward potential content contributors, they then grow a base of articles from the resulting response and they can then harvest the advertising money from it. If they fairly split profits with content contributors who write for them, this can be a good thing, in addition to providing authors with readership exposure.

Contracts that Give Websites Permanent Ownership of Articles

This chapter's title is meant to get the attention of writers/authors who are considering writing for such venues.

They can be genuinely good opportunities in some cases however, some sites offer contracts to writers that are overly-biased toward them. Some contracts for example, state that the content contributed to them by contracted author/members, becomes their property perpetually (forever) and it also cannot be removed at any point by the contributor, including for the purpose of compilation into eBooks. In some cases, this type term is also stated with exclusivity attached to it, meaning it not only belongs to the site in-question, eternally but the author cannot at any time publish any content submitted to them, any place else online, in-print or in digital form of any type. This would include placing the content on other websites or into books and eBooks as previously mentioned. Even if such a term is not exclusive to them, it may still grant a website in-question the right to permanently market your content, regardless of what you may also being doing with it at any given point in time. Some of these strict-policy websites also block authors from being able to go into their contributed articles and make changes to them, once they have passed their editorial standards and are approved for going live.

This of course also includes the inability to remove a piece at any point afterward as previously mentioned. What adds insult-to-injury, is the fact that the extended publishing of an authors content at these type content websites, may not pay any additional commissions/earnings to the author.

The ad-sharing revenue of the site (or whatever type of compensation is offered), may be restricted to that which is earned on their main website but not from any outside sources they may also market the content to. The site can then harvest the extra income without splitting a percent of it with authors.

My Negative Experience with a "How To" Property

To give an example of a website I experienced this very scenario with, I will refer to a "How To" type property (website specializing in articles on how to do certain things). They were splitting ad revenue with authors for the first couple of years they were in business but at one point, they simply decided to discontinue the revenue sharing.

Their reasoning offered, was that they were going to a different type of format for their website however, they continued to have paid-advertisers and were still a profit website. They had gleaned literally 10s of 1,000s of articles from authors before making this change to a non profit sharing site. They were the type site that also blocked the ability for authors to change or remove articles and so when this major change occurred and I was unable to remove my content from their site, I wrote them, threatening legal mediation. To my surprise, this worked, without any further action required on my part and they removed my content from their website.

Another amazing thing regarding this incident, was the fact that the site had taken author's content and they began to advertise it as little eBooks guides, on a major bookseller's website. None of the authors were told about this and we simply came across our articles, offered in eBook form, inadvertently via online search. I mentioned the fact of my having found my content for sale as eBooks, to the website administration when I had my content removed and they eventually also stopped advertising it on the bookseller site.

Their explanation for having started this added selling venture, was to say that they entered into an arrangement with an outside company who was doing the eBook marketing. Regardless, authors were seriously taken advantage of in the case of this "How To" property-website.

Some Content Websites are Good to Authors

Is there dishonesty and unfairness in the content website industry? I believe this chapter demonstrates that this is indeed the case however, this does not take away from the fact that there are honest ones out there that treat authors fairly and honestly. I believe it also demonstrates the importance in carefully considering the terms included in content contributor contracts before entering into them with these type of writer-opportunity websites.

CHAPTER EIGHT

Why I Write Short Subject Health eBooks/Books

My shorter-subject books/eBooks, are often in the approximate 6,000 word range, with some being over 12,000 words and I still consider them short subjects. I price the vast majority of them at $2.99, in order for them to be in Amazon's higher commission bracket of 70% versus 35% but they can be as high as $9.99 to meet that requirement. A range of $2.99 to $9.99 is the price range for the 70% commission category as mentioned in a previous chapter.

My First eBooks

When I first began publishing eBooks, it was at the prompting of a thyroid disease website I contributed a dozen or so articles to in year-2005, who asked if I would supply them an eBook to offer their readers. This website was in the UK and I provided them an eBook on the subject of hypothyroidism (underactive thyroid gland).

143

When the site administrator received it, he asked if I could shorten it a bit because his experience with the site and its correlating forum, brought him to realize that readers wanting some education regarding a disease they are suffering, prefer eBooks that come straight to the point regarding the facts they are seeking (I actually thought the eBook was already short in length before the editing request).

He added that many readers prefer not having to trudge through info-sources on specific subjects, that are overly-descriptive, that veer-off into tangents or that include lots of references to other info-sources the writer might have learned their information from.

The Type of Book: A Deciding Factor for Page-Length

While my next statement might be met with disagreement by readers, who are also fellow-publishers of eBooks/books that are on similar subjects I write on, in many cases, the types of lengthy info I describe above is added, simply to extend the number of pages, which is a selling-point in a book's description.

144

Do understand that I am not referring to books with several sections because in this case, each section can cover a different subject. I have a number of books that are lengthy and contain multiple sections (my lengthiest is 420 pages that are 8.5 X 11.5 in size) but this-too is understood in the book-description. I also want to make it clear that books for "pleasure reading" are **a very different story**. In this case, readers love those with lots of length to them. This would include novels and works of both fiction and non-fiction, that tell intriguing or interesting stories or that provide interesting information for the enjoyment of the reader.

Online Search and General Educational Resources (Books & eBooks)

When it comes to readers who have been newly diagnosed with a disease or health disorder of some type for example, and the typical scenario is involved in-which their doctor simply does not have the time to provide them anything more than a very scant education regarding it, many will seek further information from other sources.

Most will begin to search online, hopefully at reputable medical sources but in the old days before the popularity of the internet, they would seek their info by talking to other people suffering their same disease or they would search their local library for books on the subject. Certainly many people still do this and some do-so, in addition to conducting an online search.

The problem that sometimes arises, is that each online source one might search, may cover a subject scantly, including all of the major points and still not include the detail one is seeking that provides them a better, **general education** regarding a disease they are suffering. I'm still not referring to information that is so intense that it would be equal to that needed to earn a master's degree on the subject but thorough-enough and with the needed-detail, to satisfy their need to be as educated as a layperson (non-professional) can be. I will admit that this can be a difficult balance to strike for an author of disease/health subjects and it's unlikely that any of us have ever done so to absolute perfection. We have to proceed with the details of a written-work, as our hearts lead us.

This includes how we feel about book/eBook length, based on our experiences with the reading public and what we have learned from other authors and content source administrators (i.e. websites and forums).

Experience Equals Writing Methods

I formerly served as a forum moderator for patient support of those with thyroid diseases, at several websites (including being topic editor for one of the connected websites) and a common complaint I saw and one that was actually directed at my own posts on occasion, was that they were too-lengthy. I tend to be a very detailed person and fellow forum members would at times tell me that they preferred not to see long blocks of information or ones that included too-much detail or that were loaded-down with too much medically technical language.

I actually had doctors who wrote me, asking how I treated my patients who had certain types of diseases or symptoms and I had to let them know that I am not a medical professional or a doctor of any type but rather a well-studied layperson.

The combination of all of these experiences helped me to arrive at decisions regarding the length of disease-subject eBooks I wrote from that point forward and the style of information they contain.

I have since written many short subject eBooks, plus, for those readers who do prefer lengthier books that cover all related subjects within a main-heading, I have also written a number of those type. So-far, my short subjects ones, on a book-by-book basis, have had a higher response by about a 10 to 1 ratio. Strangely enough, I occasionally have a reader post a review under one of my eBook titles, saying it was "too-short" and so here we have the diversity of types of readers that sometimes manifests. I suppose in these cases, the famous saying attributed to Abraham Lincoln can be referred-to: *"You can please some of the people all of the time and all of the people some of the time but you can't please all of the people all of the time."*

Apparently the advice I received from the UK website administrator back in about year-2005, has largely proven to be the case.

This is true at least in regard to the genre of disease subjects I have written about but desired book-lengths vary greatly to consumers, depending on the genre or subject-matter that is covered by them.

It is my hope that the advice I have offered within this chapter and within the preceding ones, including the occasional "rants and raves", have provided some nuggets of sound information, for consideration by the readers of them!

(END - SECTION THREE)

SECTION FOUR

Corrupt Business Practices in Newspaper Circulation

The Eye-opening Experiences of a Newsboy

Dedicated to all of the honest, hard working newspaper carriers throughout the world.

TABLE OF CONTENTS (SECTION FOUR):

INTRODUCTION - SECTION FOUR:

While this 4th section of the book, is not actually on the subject of indie authoring or publishing, it does relate to it indirectly because some independent authors do indeed write as freelancers for in-print newspapers. I also believe the experiences I relate regarding dishonestly within a newspaper I worked as a distribution agent for, further helps to educate readers, in regard to the types of scams that are perpetrated by those who are dishonest within the publishing world in general.

 Understanding that these types of things do happen, can help us to stay on our toes so-to-speak, in protecting our own interests, whether they be in the writing, marketing or distribution areas of the publishing field.

(Note: Neither the name of the publishing company I make reference to nor any of its employees or representatives will be named in this book.)

During the decades starting in the 1980s and into the first decade of the 2000s, I worked for four different newspaper and magazine publications.

This includes my being hired as a district manager for one of them – a position I held for only a couple of weeks (more on this story later). Even people, who know me personally, will not be able to determine with certainty, which newspaper publication I will be referring-to, regarding corrupt business practices that I will describe as being perpetrated by them. In my opinion, it doesn't matter at this point, who the company was. What ultimately matters, is that people working for companies either as employees or under contracts with them, should be willing to stand up for their rights under the laws of the United States and that legislation continues to allow the opportunity for Americans to reasonably register complaints for investigation when necessary. In-short, dishonest business practices should be exposed for what they are.

Legitimate Complaints

Certainly a reasonable degree of screening must also occur, so that bogus complaints by irate, disgruntled or vindictive employees are not given undue credence. Those with legitimate complaints however, that are well-documented should not feel intimidated against registering these when necessary.

They should also not be made to feel that simply wanting to see accountability for corrupt business practices by a company, with no further personal gain sought by them, is going to come at a personal financial cost to them. They should also not feel they are in danger of reprisals by a company or by those directly or indirectly associated with them for registering a legitimate complaint. It should also be recognized that employees can be the source of corruption in a company as well and can be guilty of cheating their employers. Opportunity for companies to seek accountability in these cases is equally important.

Seeking Remedies

I did take a degree of action by registering complaints against the company I refer-to in this book, through a mediating bureau. This was the only amount of time I was willing to invest in attempt to see possible accountability result and changes that might result from it. My reason for reluctance in taking further action was based on the fact that I have seen far too-much unwillingness on the part of others affected by unethical business behaviors to seek remedies for them.

Collaboration is often essential in cases such as mine that I will describe in the chapters that follow but the cooperation by those of like-complaints was simply not available to me.

This brought me to the realization that most people affected by corrupt business practices would rather simply walk away from them afterward, as opposed to "getting involved" in trying to change them or to bring accountability to companies for perpetrating them. This, despite the fact that we don't attempt to influence changes only for the sake of ourselves but also for the sake of others who might also be affected.

My Inspiration for this Book

In some ways I regret not having done more in my case, after so many years of witnessing this type of thing which is largely the inspiration behind this book.

I also feel that the type practices I will describe that included illegitimate methods for increasing circulation by some newspaper companies, is far more common than the general public may realize.

This also means that the cost of advertising being purchased from these newspapers, by businesses and consumers is sometimes illegitimately inflated by dishonest companies, based on false circulation numbers. Could it be that this is possibly one of the reasons for the continuing downfall of printed newspapers, with honest ones suffering, along with the dishonest ones?

It often takes collaborating experiences to get the attention of those who investigate and prosecute or penalize illegal business activities, such as those I have just described. In many cases, those who try to get the ball rolling on an investigation of a company, will find their selves alone and are afterward pegged as "whistle blowers".

This is unfortunate and the very reason these type business practices continue in companies and often progressively increase when accountability is lacking. I believe this "ripple effect" – if you will, affects all types of businesses to some degree and also those who are in public office positions, from small town governments to the higher offices of government service.

Recognizing Honest Businessmen

At the same time, there are many honest and highly ethical people in these businesses, and offices, including those in the newspaper industry but honesty can only maintain an upper-hand when accountability for potential dishonestly remains in place and is practiced when necessary. It is my belief as a Christian and believer in a God who judges the actions of all men and women that accountability does eventually occur as a result of what we might call "the reaping process" even when accountability within a company is lacking. It is my personal belief that not one person escapes the reward or the punishment for both the good and evil practices they commit during their lifetimes. Some believers in the inescapable and inevitable process of judgment and reward simply refer to it using the term "justice prevails" and I am certainly a believer of this statement.

In the chapters of this book that follow, I will relate my experiences as a contract carrier for a newspaper, during which time I witnessed an alarming frequency of corrupt business practices that in many cases directly affected me and my family as well as fellow contract workers and employees of the company.

CHAPTER ONE

Why I became a Newsboy

Being a newspaper distributor is something I would have never guessed earlier in my life, to be an occupation I would eventually hold for over 16 years however, life-circumstances, including some very positive ones, brought me to the eventual destiny of becoming a "newsboy".

My duties on the job included distribution of newspapers to stores and newspaper racks, in addition to home subscribers. The only difficult aspect of the job, was the detailed paperwork involved in keeping singly copy circulation (outlet sales) and home delivery subscriber circulation recorded as well as a record of unsold newspapers (returns) for which I was given credit. Surprisingly, the income for this occupation was quite good, which gave me ample daytime hours to successfully pursue the marketing of a fishing tackle accessory, product-invention and to further my writing profession. Despite this fact, there were many times I found myself having to battle corrupt business practices that in some cases negatively affected my own income by 1,000s of dollars.

This often required my relentless persistence to see correction of them and past-due credit balances paid back to me.

My Former Occupations

In the year 1989, I formed a small corporation in my hometown to market a fishing tackle accessory that I invented in partnership with my brother-in-law. I involved local businessmen who agreed to finance the product-invention, so that it would be under a patent pending status, placed in packaging for retail sales and properly covered by product liability insurance, required by major retail chain stores and outlets.

I was a specialty foods salesman at the time, working many hours and traveling 100s of miles per week, which made it difficult to invest the time that was needed to successfully market the product invention.

My wife was also pregnant at the time, with our second child – a daughter, who would be born in 1990. The pregnancy was a difficult one however, with my wife suffering premature dilation of her cervix and frequent contractions that began occurring early into her pregnancy.

As a result, she was required to undergo a medical procedure called a "cervical cerclage" to prevent premature birth of our daughter. The procedure was successful and our daughter who is now pursuing a master's degree in a medical pathology field was born full-term.

I was able to secure regional distribution for the fishing accessory in Wal-Mart stores and I landed a promotion for the product with a major oil company who used the product to increase sales of their outboard motor oil by placing a unit in each case they manufactured. These sales gave us corporate capitol to increase our marketing and I began being paid a small monthly salary by the corporation. My partners knew that my time was valuable and that I needed ample time during normal business hours, to promote the product and to increase sales by continued representation of the product to new outlets and to remain in contact with those already carrying it. Not long afterward, I also secured distribution for the product through Bass Pro Shops, Cabela's and Academy Stores. We eventually licensed the product to a large fishing tackle conglomerate – TTI Blakemore Corporation, who still pays us monthly royalties from sales that accrue through these same outlets.

A Perfect Fit

I resigned my position with the specialty food company and looked for work I could perform on-the-side, during hours that would not affect the marketing of the fishing tackle accessory. I found an ad by a publishing company, seeking a contract newspaper distributor and I was hired to perform the early morning deliveries and the associated paperwork during available hours when I was not involved in the product marketing. It was a perfect fit and over time, I actually began to enjoy the newspaper distribution position.

160

CHAPTER TWO

Collection Time Shenanigans

After being interviewed for the contract newspaper carrier position, at my home, by the District Manager (DM), I was hired for the position.

I remember upon first showing up at the site where newspapers were dropped each morning, to be disbursed by carriers, that several of them approached me, warning that the DM was extremely dishonest and that he would take every possible opportunity to cheat you out of money.

They also added that the main office knew about his corrupt practices but that they had no intention of firing him or reprimanding him for them because he was achieving circulation increases for the company. I did not believe the accusations and I came to the conclusion at the time, that these were simply carriers who were disgruntled with the company for whatever reasons. At the end of my first month of contract services as a newspaper carrier for the company, the DM came to collect from me.

He would have me pay the difference between
what I had collected from my customers, versus
what I owed the company once my unsold
newspapers were credited off of the balance due.
He calculated these figures and computed the
amount I owed the company for the current month
due and asked me to pay him cash. This struck me
a bit strange and so I asked him why he was
asking for a cash-payment. He replied by saying
that it simply made it easier for him to pay the
main office a lump sum he would collect from all
carriers combined, rather than having to take a
number of different personal checks back to the
main office with him. This sounded logical and
my wife and I agreed to pay the cash to settle our
first month's bill. Afterward however, we decided
that it was better for us to have a canceled check
for tax-record purposes and that when he came
back on the next month's collection date, we
would simply tell him this.

An Emerging Pattern of Dishonesty

When the next end-of-month rolled around, we
explained this to the DM and he agreed but he
then asked if we would make checks payable to
his name, rather than to the company's name.

With a second strange request being made I began to feel uncomfortable but I agreed to the request, since he was willing to accept a check, rather than cash. Being a new contract carrier, I didn't understand the newspaper business well enough to recognize that this was not a proper way for the DM to collect from me. What really placed me on alert however, was the fact that within days of my making the payment to him, he arrived at my home claiming he had made a mistake during the collections and that he needed an additional sum of money (relatively small) to turn in to the main office, to completely settle my balance-due. He also added that he had made up for the difference out of his own pocket and needed the payment for reimbursement.

I again agreed to make the payment but by this time I had developed a strong mistrust for this DM. While looking at a past statement, I found written in small print at the bottom of it, directions stating to the effect that contract carriers were to make checks payable, only to the company. This gave me further substantiation for the feelings of mistrust I had developed for this man.

Looking Out for my Interests

I began to understand my statement better in-
general, involving newspapers provided me and
credits applied to my bill, leaving the difference I
would owe each month. I began to go over these
with a fine toothed comb so-to-speak, to make
sure that the amount the DM collected from me
was also the amount he was actually turning in to
the main office. About one year later, the manager
over the circulation department and this DM's
boss called me, asking if I would take a DM
position that was open in another area but with
my other responsibilities at the time, I politely
refused the job (it would be offered to me again
later).

While I was on the phone with him however, I
mentioned that the DM who was collecting from
me, was having me make my checks payable to
him. The circulation manager immediately
pointed out that this is not what he was supposed
to be doing and that I could refuse to do so if I
wished. I was floored when he added that this
same DM was caught skimming money from
collections that were due to the company.

This required him to pay the company back on two previous occasions for money he had basically embezzled.

Increasing Circulation Covers a Multitude of Sins

This corrupt DM was also known for turning-in many new customer orders, increasing subscriber circulation and winning yearly contests among his peers for doing-so and this apparently was the reason the company allowed the questionable practices to continue for years following. The company did however require the DM to repay monies he had obtained from them illegally but they did not appear to be concerned about monies he had cheated carriers out of during that same period of time. This brings me to another unethical practice this DM was involved in that I will cover in the next chapter and one that the company would not resolve, in spite of numerous complaints from many carriers over several years period of time.

CHAPTER THREE

Tucked Away for a Rainy Day

Performing the duties of a newspaper carrier requires use of delivery supplies, including rubber bands and plastic bags to protect newspapers delivered during wet weather conditions. This is true of both home subscriber customers and stores that are delivered early mornings before they have opened for business. These supplies were sold to carriers by the newspaper company as they needed them with the cost of the supplies being applied to their monthly statements.

Fellow contract carriers began to approach me frequently, claiming that supplies they had not ordered nor received were showing up as charges on their monthly statements, sometimes amounting to 100s of dollars.

Eventually, the same thing happened to me as well and I questioned the DM about it. He responded by saying that the supplies were some I had ordered months previously and that the main office had somehow failed to make the appropriate charges at the time.

Oh what a Tangled Web we Weave

I accepted this explanation being given by the DM at the time however, within a month or two of these charges being explained to me, I ordered new supplies. Upon these being delivered to me by the DM, he asked that I pay for them by cash or check, rather than charges for them being applied to my upcoming statement.

He added that this is how the company wanted him to handle supplies being sold to contract carriers for the time being. I decided this time, that I would call someone in management at the circulation department to confirm that I was actually supposed to pay for the supplies upfront. I was told that they were unaware of any such directive being given to DMs regarding supplies to contract carriers, which confirmed my suspicion that this was not supposed to be occurring.

An Insult to the Intelligence

It was not difficult to figure out the type of scam that was being perpetrated and in some ways; these types of issues were insulting to one's intelligence.

Apparently, there is the belief by some in the newspaper business, that contract carriers are people who lack intelligence or who come from a very low-class background. While this certainly can be the case (regardless of occupation), I personally worked with fellow contract carriers who were well-known retired businessmen or who were police officers or managers of other businesses and delivered newspapers as supplemental jobs.

In regard to the bogus supplies charges, the DM was simply signing for supplies at the main office and applying charges for them, to carriers who had not actually ordered them. He would then take the supplies that would be paid-for via these charges and would re-sell them to other carriers for cash payments. While I did not confront the DM with this revelation specifically, I did tell him that I would no longer pay for supplies upfront but that I would require that they be applied as charges to my monthly statements. I also added that I intended to keep up with my supply orders very closely.

Amazingly, this was all it took to stop the bogus charges from intermittently showing up on my monthly statements.

A new type of bogus charge eventually began showing up on carrier's monthly statements however that not only added potential bonus compensation to the DM but that also increased newspaper circulation numbers illegitimately.

In addition to this, a newly-devised plan involving discontinued home subscriber customers also began to occur. I will give detail to these other scams that were being perpetrated, to benefit both the income and circulation of the publishing company, in chapters that follow.

Outfoxing the Fox

It began to appear as if new scams were continually being devised as old ones were being figured-out by the contract carriers. Our main defenses against these practices were to either resign our contracts (which many did) or to watch our monthly statements very closely and to go over them in detail to catch any bogus activity that might be occurring on them.

I chose the latter approach because the work fit-well into my other activities and I did not want to be a quitter.

The job was also one of self-employment and logically required diligence in self-representation of the contract-carrier side of the business agreement. Being self-employed requires a degree of self-advocacy in order to survive these types of issues.

CHAPTER FOUR

How to Increase Newspaper Circulation without even Trying

With my being the carrier with the largest delivery territory, the publishing company required a few extra duties of me. They placed a toll-free number telephone in my home, so that I could take complaints from customers who missed their deliveries or who were seeking subscriber information. I also handed-out any complaints to fellow carriers that came in on the phone line, each previous morning. At one point, carriers began to complain frequently that newspapers were not being discontinued from their daily count, even after they had turned-in delivery stops on them. These were those who failed to pay their delivery bill or who had moved or passed away, etc...

Delivering Newspapers to the Dead

Some of the carriers were showing me discontinued subscribers, no longer being delivered, mounting up into the dozens, even with repeated stops being placed on them, via proper paperwork and phone calls to the main office.

171

I eventually asked the DM why this was occurring and he stated that the main office was not allowing stops at that time because they wanted to achieve an increase over the previous year's circulation. The only problem with this plan was the fact that the carriers were still being charged for these customers, which in some cases added 100s of dollars to their statements each month. Some carriers actually resigned over the issue as others did due to other past issues involving dishonesty in the company.

The DM devised a solution to this problem but one I was very uncomfortable with. Since my routes included those that I delivered to single copy customers (stores and news racks) and since I was reimbursed for any unsold newspapers, I could simply turn-in these carrier's undelivered newspapers on my paperwork for credit, so that they would no longer be paying for them. At the same time, home subscriber circulation would not decrease. This was the instruction I received from the DM and that he had me to continue doing over the next three years. I asked him when this first began, if he would take responsibility for instructing the carriers to turn these in to me and he assured me that he would.

172

I also called the man who was zone manager at the time and asked him if I should be following this instruction by the DM and he told me to continue following the instructions.

Documentation... Documentation... Documentation!

Despite this fact, in order to safeguard against blame being shifted to me should the practice be investigated at any point, I asked each carrier to sign a sheet stating to the effect that they were turning these undelivered newspapers over to me for credit at the DM's instruction. I also saved all canceled checks I paid to each carrier, which amounted to 1,000s of dollars over a three year period. I eventually complained enough about the length of time that this practice was being continued that the DM finally agreed to place stops on discontinued customers for these carriers rather than continuing the home subscriber circulation scam.

Not long following discontinuation of paying for carrier's undelivered newspapers, a new scam emerged, this time directly affecting income-credit due to single copy carriers.

We were in-essence being cheated out of income due to us for our delivery services to stores and news racks (single copy sales). The DM and whoever else was involved in this scam began "charging back" carriers for unsold newspapers, turned-in by them at the end of each month for credit.

Carriers would turn in their unsold newspapers, logging them onto a sheet that calculated the amount of credit due to them that would be subtracted from their monthly statements.

Carriers with single copy sales on their routes began to complain to me, that they were being charged-back for unsold newspapers they were turning in and I responded by letting them know that the same thing was happening to me as well.

When Honesty is not Welcome

It was during this time that a new DM was assigned over the area that included my routes and those of these other carriers. This man was refreshingly honest in his practices and he showed genuine concern for what was occurring regarding the charge-backs.

When I mentioned the complaints I was hearing from other carriers, he stated that carriers throughout his district were being charged-back for returns, for several months running, with the implied reason being that the main office was finding discrepancies in the numbers of unsold newspapers being turned in.

We both agreed that this many carriers could not possibly all be giving incorrect calculations for several consecutive months and that this appeared to be a bogus method for increasing single copy circulation. Some of these carriers were adamant that they were not miscounting returns in their own favor and that in some cases they recounted them several times or had a family member recount them for accuracy before turning them in.

The new DM and his Zone Manager (also an honest man), decided that they would run an experiment on the issue, using my returns and those of other carrier's on the test. When they came to collect my next month's returns, they would personally count them, before turning them over to the main office, to see if they would still show a discrepancy and a charge-back.

Amazingly, the charge-backs did appear again and this was confirmation to these managers that there was indeed a scam involving bogus charge-backs occurring. Not long following this incident, the Zone Manager resigned his job and the DM was fired from his.

These two men were not the only honest employees who worked for the publishing company but who resigned or were fired due to issues of dishonesty they were witnessing. There was another DM, who was promoted to a Zone Management position as well, who also eventually resigned with the newspaper after many months of attempting to convince the heads of the company to correct the methods of dishonesty that were occurring.

As I write this chapter, I recall receiving an email from this man, just last week, in which he reminded me that he could no longer continue with a company whose standard was that of deceit. I admire him for taking the stance that he did, as these other men did. I believe much of what drove this man's convictions of honesty are centered in the fact that he is a Christian man (now a full time Minister) and retired from honorable service with the U.S. military.

An Offer I couldn't Refuse

There was a point in time in which I-too resigned within two weeks of being hired for a DM position and afterward I returned to a contract delivery position. The turnover of both contract carrier and management positions was incredibly frequent and logically, this was due to the issues that were occurring within the company. I literally saw a dozen DMs come and go in less than two years at one point and my own reason for resigning was due to yet another issue of dishonesty as well.

I was offered a district management territory that included several cities with relatively large populations within it. A number of DMs who had resigned the district complained that it was too large and impossible for one person to handle. I was notified of the position and offered the district with one of the larger cities being taken off of it.

The circulation manager, who hired me, even stated that with the district being reduced in size, it would be far less of a headache for a new DM.

I accepted the position under the revised circumstances and once I was fully trained, I was informed that the city was added back into the district. I basically felt as if I was tricked into accepting the position and I resigned it as a result. Amazingly, they called me a short time later, asking if I would take a contract delivery territory for which I agreed. It was obvious that the company often operated in a mode of desperation due to the frequency of managers and carriers resigning.

CHAPTER FIVE

Confessions of a Corrupt District Manager

As mentioned previously, the first DM I witnessed perpetrating dishonest business practices was eventually fired from his job. The company had apparently allowed his corrupt behaviors to the fullest extent possible but once enough fingers began to be pointed at the company itself, it was time for a little housecleaning. There was also likely the fear that a DM would have the ability to implement other company representatives as holding some responsibility for their dishonest practices.

Prior to his being fired, the DM began to run routes that were resigned by carriers, while keeping the monthly pay customer payments as personal profit. Company policy did not allow DMs to keep monies received from down routes but it was to be turned-in to a company fund. The DM found a way around this policy by making it appear that a carrier was contracted on a down route, while he himself was actually delivering it.

179

At times, I was the carrier he showed to be on a down route, while he received the profits from it and I eventually discovered this rather inadvertently.

The DM would approach me early mornings while I was picking up my newspapers at the drop-site and he would ask me to sign a blank contract. He claimed that my original contract was misplaced at the main office and that this would place it back on file. I was highly suspicious of this request due to his past behaviors but I agreed to sign the contract. A few days later he appeared at my home to inform me that he sent out bills to monthly pay customers on a down route and that he used my name and address for them to remit payment to. He asked that I cash the checks as they came in and turn the payments over to him.

How about a little Tax Evasion?

I immediately figured out what he was doing and I asked him if he realized that I would have to report the income as my own and pay taxes on it at the end of the year.

His answer in-response to this question was that I shouldn't report it and with the income actually not belonging to me, I didn't report it. While the payments totaled just under $1,000.00 this still amounted to yet one more feather in his hat of corruption, being that of tax evasion, in addition to breaking company policy, among other things. There were times I would be in phone conversation with the circulation manager and he would thank me for filling-in on down routes to help the DM between finding new carriers. These were down routes I knew for a fact I had not filled in on.

A few weeks prior to the DM being asked to leave the company, I was standing alone with him in my front yard and I basically asked him why he committed so much dishonesty in his business practices. He literally displayed a look of regret on his face as he opened-up to me and began to admit that he was involved in a great deal of corruption and that the company was allowing it, as long as he kept the circulation numbers increased in his district. He further answered my question by saying that he struggled with an anguishing fear that he would not make enough money and as a result that he might lose his wife.

He added that he found a number of ways to insure that he made sufficient income. I was shocked by the fact that he was confessing this to me but at the same time I had no sympathy for him whatsoever and found no legitimacy in his excuse.

Amazingly, a circulation manager who had somewhat befriended me, after my many years as a contract carrier for the company, made a similar admission to me by phone on one occasion.

Knowing I was a Christian, he stated to me that he regretted many of the things he had resorted to in his business practices with the company. I only hope these same confessions were offered to the ears of God and that true repentance followed them, especially with the fact that he-too was a professing Christian.

Shortly before my wife and I resigned our contracts with the company, she happened to be speaking to this same circulation manager on the phone regarding issues we were experiencing. He made a statement to us that again came as somewhat of a shock.

In reference to the fact that the company was beginning to struggle to meet budgets and were feverishly finding every possible avenue to increase revenues, including downsizing their work force, he simply stated to her that we should "watch our backs" (verbatim quote). This was his way of indirectly warning us that we could be on the receiving end of further corrupt activities. Within months of that phone call, we resigned due to credit balances due to us being withheld and delayed, which permanently ended our association with the company.

CHAPTER SIX

Ghost Routes Galore

As economic changes and internet availability of news began to negatively affect printed newspaper companies, many of them began to downsize their delivery areas and their base of employees. The newspaper I served as contract carrier for was no exception and one of the first things to go with their downsizing efforts were "rural customers" (those outside of city limits). There were a number of rural routes discontinued, just outside of the areas where I was delivering to customers in the suburbs.

The company apparently had a brainstorm and decided to devise a plan that would allow them to continue showing these customers from the discontinued routes, as being current ones, to prevent a reduction in home subscriber circulation numbers. They simply added the names and addresses of these customers from the discontinued routes, to my monthly statements. The newspapers themselves were stopped and were not being sent out to be delivered but the paperwork showed that they were.

Each of these rural customers would be listed on my monthly statements, including charges to me for the newspapers I was not getting, for over a year and a half following discontinued delivery to them. The new DM at the time, informed me that the company had made these same type revisions by adding discontinued rural customers to other carrier's lists in his district.

A Purposeful Glitch in the System

When this manipulation of the rural customer lists first began to occur and upon my complaining about it to the main office, I was told that it was a temporary development that was occurring due to changes in their accounting system but that it would soon be resolved. This again was seemingly an insult to my intelligence because customers from a different route, that are all under different route-numbers and contract carrier's names, do not transfer to other routes unless done-so intentionally. It was also obvious that the scam was being perpetrated in order to prevent a sudden and significant reduction in circulation numbers.

This was especially obvious with the fact that this continued for over 18 months.

A new DM was placed over the district and he began attempting to get the issue resolved because it was negatively affecting my credit balance by 100s of dollars per month and these charges for rural customer newspapers were not being credited back to me. When the past credit due to me and my wife who had also been delivering routes by that time for approximately five years and who also had rural customers added to her statements reached over $4,000.00, we let the new DM know that we would be resigning as a result of it. He then decided to send a memo directly to the circulation manager, detailing these bogus charges and requesting that we be issued checks to cover them, immediately, in exchange for us remaining under contract.

Resolved by a Memo

This was not the first time the circulation manager was informed of the issue, in-fact I had personally spoken to him about it as well but the memo was the step that succeeded (I still retain a copy of it) and we were finally compensated for the bogus rural customer charges.

While the company corrected the issue with us, this still does not take away from the fact that a dishonest circulation scam was taking place and that the publishing company was not held accountable for their unethical business practices.

As mentioned in my introduction, I firmly believe that accountability for dishonest actions is sometimes delayed but never escaped. While I personally hold no grudge against any of these individuals I am also confident in divine judgment. My personal hope is that these individuals have repented of their deeds and are moving forward in honest pursuits and this I state with absolute sincerely.

The Last Straw

Some months following correction of the previously described issue involving scam circulation increases, other issues began to develop, affecting both my mine and my wife's credit balances as contract carriers. Once again, this was tantamount to taking food out of our family's mouths. I had warned the company that if such issues began to occur again, that we would resign our contracts without notice and this is what eventually occurred.

Normally, early resignation without proper notice will bring a penalty/fine to a contract carrier, according to the company's policies. Upon our resignation, I firmly suggested that the company accept a "clean break" from us; in addition to paying us for all past-due credit balances we were owed. They did abide by the request which we forwarded to them through a mediating bureau and they resolved the issue on an immediate basis. Their promptness was almost certainly due to the fact that I warned of further reporting to additional agencies should they have not accepted our terms of resignation.

CONCLUSION:

I am not so naive as to not recognize that corruption in business has always existed and will continue to exist throughout this dispensation of mankind. I do however believe that the legal avenues in-place that provides opportunity to remedy some of these issues is often not resorted-to. I must point a finger of guilt at myself in this regard because I failed to act sooner and as often as I should have. In many cases it is simply a matter of victims not wanting to experience the stress of reporting illegal practices.

For others it may be a matter of not really caring about issues of dishonestly being perpetrated in business if it does not directly affect them. Fear of reprisals as previously mentioned is yet another reason businesses may not be called into accountability by observers of their unethical behaviors.

The Leaven of Corruption

Regardless of the reasons corruption may be allowed to continue within companies, this often gives it opportunity to grow and continue to increase in incidence, which can eventually affect societies as a whole. A very wise man once said *"A little leaven leavens the whole lump of dough."* – meaning the yeast of corruption, when left to work, can eventually take over the whole ball of dough. It is my hope that the preceding chapters of this book help to inspire others to step forward in self-advocacy against dishonest business practices and to also do-so on the behalf of others who might eventually be affected by it. When honest people join together to bring about accountability for corrupt business practices, changes can take place and differences made.

(END)

www.ingramcontent.com/pod-product-compliance
Lightning Source LLC
Chambersburg PA
CBHW051502170526
45166CB00001B/350